THE 3 CEOs
FORMULA

THE 3 CEOs FORMULA

For Building Success & Wealth in Network Marketing and Life

Floyd Williams,
Spencer Iverson
and Donald Bradley

The 3 CEOs, LLC

Three CEOs Formula:
For Building Success and Wealth in Network Marketing and Life
Copyright © 2008 by Floyd Williams, Spencer Iverson and Donald Bradley
Published by The 3 CEOs, LLC

For further information, please contact:
www.thethreeceos.com

Printed in the United States of America

Three CEOs Formula:
For Building Success and Wealth in Network Marketing and Life
Floyd Williams, Spencer Iverson and Donald Bradley

1. Title 2. Author 3. Business Strategy

Library of Congress Control Number: 2008905489

ISBN-10: 0-9818662-0-4
ISBN-13: 978-0-9818662-0-8

In loving memory of Anthony Jones,
an unsung hero.

Table of Contents

Acknowledgments

Floyd

I would like to first thank God for His guidance and blessing, which allowed me to make my contribution to this book. It is my hope that the content of it will bless someone as it has richly blessed me.

Second, I would like to thank my beautiful wife, who is my number-one partner and best friend. Love ya, Carla baby, and thanks for your unconditional love and support.

Thank you to my Mom, Ms. Loretta Williams, for her love, guidance and admiration. To my late father, Mr. Floyd Williams, Sr., I love you, Dad, and miss you much.

Thanks to my kids, Carmen and Jordan, my precious gifts from God.

To my two brothers, Tim Williams and Dennis Williams, thanks for your support and love.

And last but not least, thanks to my partners in business,

Spencer Iverson and Donald Bradley. What a journey! You guys are simply the best, and we've only just begun.

Spencer

God has truly blessed my life in more ways than I could ever count and has brought me through some very dark times. So, thank You, God, for Your grace and mercy, and for the gifts You have given me.

I thank my parents, John and Patricia Iverson. You are my inspiration and role models and I only hope to be half the parents to my children that you are to me. I love you.

I want to thank my late grandparents, Fermon and Bessie Spencer. I miss you guys so much.

To my gorgeous wife, Tonya: You have stood by my side through all the crazy ideas, inventions, empty bank accounts and new businesses. Thank you for your patience and belief in me.

I thank my wonderful kids, Brandon Spencer and Hayley Nicole. Daddy is sorry for being gone so much; thank you for understanding and giving me those great hugs when I come home.

To my brothers and sisters, John, Margaret, Ivan, Janelle and Patrick: God could not have picked a better family to place me in. Thank you for your unwavering and genuine love and support.

I want to thank my two church families, the Southside Church of Christ in Valdosta, Georgia, and the West End Church of Christ in Atlanta, Georgia. Thank you for your spiritual support and for nurturing my family and me.

I must thank the thousands and thousands of team members in our organization around the world who work tirelessly to reach their dreams through our leadership. May this book give you inspiration and hope.

I want to thank my dear friend, Randall Godfrey. You are like a brother to me and I thank you for your friendship through the years. You know that Diedra is somewhere, beaming with pride at the men we have become.

I want to thank Lloyd "Coach" Tomer, Scott Tomer and Kim Sorenson for building a business model that makes sense and gives everyone a chance to reach their financial dreams.

Finally, it must have been destiny, but God gave me two of the best business partners I could ever imagine. Floyd and Don, you guys are two more big brothers to me. It's about time that the rest of the world samples your brilliance. Thanks for pushing me to be better than I ever dreamed. This has been one crazy, fun and incredible ride! What's next?!

Donald

I want to thank my parents, Charles and Doris Bradley, and my wife and kids.

Preface

Finding one successful businessperson is pretty easy these days. Finding two people with the ability and willingness to share information that will cultivate leadership and inspire greatness is not so common. Finding three individuals with different backgrounds working together toward the same end can only be considered a phenomenon.

Throughout history, the number three has been shrouded in mystery and revered for its significance, and within our organization, we regard it with the same respect. As three individuals, as three successful entrepreneurs and business owners, we use our inherent gifts to create and administrate systems that can help ordinary people achieve extraordinary results.

Known internationally as The 3 CEOs, our unique blend of practical, inspirational and informational methods, coupled with our collective forty-plus years of entrepreneurial experience, has earned us millions of dollars. Born from our individual stories, our collective success has made us one of the most documented and successful trios in the history of network marketing.

Who We Are

Our individuality is what makes our collective effort so strong. The events and accomplishments of our separate lives have made us who we are—and have brought success to everything we've done.

Floyd Williams owned and operated a marketing and advertising agency for more than ten years before launching an extremely lucrative mortgage company. In his career, he trained thousands of people in relationship marketing and developed a national reputation as a mentor and an expert in the field.

Spencer Iverson attended law school then represented professional athletes in the National Football League and Major League Baseball, as well as golfers and basketball players, for more than ten years. At twenty-three, he was awarded a patent on an idea for a unique toothpick called Promopick, which advertised restaurants and businesses. He also invented a basketball goal for the visually impaired. He later founded a publicly traded marketing company that developed unique templates for delivering political campaigns and sports highlights via streaming audio and video on the Internet.

Donald Bradley quickly distinguished himself as a top seller in the beauty industry while also developing his own line of health and beauty products. This success led him to develop one of the leading hair care publications in the country—*Metrostyles Magazine*. Donald's skills as a promoter rounded out his talents, and helped him build a business empire.

Floyd and Spencer, long-time friends and fellow church members, met Don by chance, at a meeting about a business opportunity. The three of us developed an instant bond and soon began traveling the country together, going to meetings, making connections, and using our combined skills and talents to build one of the most successful teams in the company's history.

At one of these meetings, we met a man who seemed awed by our shared insight into building a successful business. He dubbed us the 3 CEOs, and we liked how it sounded—it said that we were three in-charge individuals, working together to make things happen. Since that day, the name has stuck.

Why Our Approach Works

When we first began writing this book, we intended to teach readers how to achieve success by working in teams of three—as we had done and continue to do. But soon, we saw the futility in that. To start with, it wasn't just our *number* that brought us success; it was our *selves*, what we each brought to the table, that made it all work. We also realized that any three people could get together, come up with a catchy name and promote themselves, even if they had no individual talents whatsoever. Would it guarantee them success? In most cases, probably not.

So, we had to stop and look at what has made The 3 CEOs a success—at what advice we really had to offer our readers. And what we discovered was that although we are totally different from each other, we've been wise enough to embrace our differences and use them, along with our many similarities, to build the strongest business structure known to man: a pyramid. A solid, three-sided structure with balanced components that rely upon each other to work.

In this book, we will explore network marketing using the three sides of a pyramid as an illustration. First, we'll take a quick look at what network marketing is, for those of you who are not familiar, and then we'll dive right into the three aspects of it that we feel are most important: leadership, action and drive. Within each of these topics, each of us will present his own opinions and advice—the 3 CEOs tackling the three sides of the pyramid, if you will.

Introduction

Traditional marketing is defined as the movement of a product or service from conception to consumption in the marketplace. The end goals are creating continuous demand and generating profits.

With *network marketing*, although the end goal is the same, the system is uniquely different. Similar to traditional marketing, network marketing serves to accomplish three key objectives: desirability, awareness and availability of a product or service. However, unlike traditional marketing, there are no advertising campaigns, radio spots or TV commercials to accomplish this objective. The network marketing business model relies solely upon word of mouth or referral-based advertising.

Network marketing companies enroll associates or reps to take the marketing message to their families, friends, business associates and all others in their circle of influence. Today, using simple, Internet-based systems, the associate or rep of a network marketing company can not only deliver the marketing message, but can close the sale and handle distribution without having to inventory a single product. This turnkey, grassroots business system allows network marketing companies to get as close to the consumer as humanly possible with a customized advertisement, delivered many times over by someone with whom they already have a relationship. Even some of the largest corporations in the world are finding it difficult to resist this streamlined business model.

In addition to getting compensated for their own direct sales of products or services, marketing reps can recruit other reps and thus build their own teams or organizations, which allows them to earn leveraged commissions from the efforts of others. Essentially, each marketing rep begins to build their own business within the overall networking marketing company of which they are a part.

Typically, getting started with a network marketing company involves a small, upfront investment that will allow you to operate under the umbrella of the company with which you're enrolled. You can then begin to use that company's "system" for recruiting other people.

How do you build this system? By getting your friends, family, acquaintances and associates involved. Or, you can bring in people you don't know at all, but who have the talent, drive and motivation to help get the job done and make your team a success. You can talk about it to people you meet at seminars or other events, in airports or in restaurants; you can meet and recruit people virtually anywhere!

As you recruit, these people become a part of your team and you reap a part of every profit they make. In turn, they can bring their own associates onboard to become members of *their* teams, and the reps get their own share of the profits from that. This is a major part of the business of network marketing; the more people you have in your organization, the more potential income there is for you.

Though, let us rephrase that: The more *quality* people you have in your organization, the greater your profits will be. A big team is nice, but it means nothing if they're not good at what they do. And how good your team is depends on the skills they have, their drive and even how well you've coached them to do the best work they can. Recruiting, training and retaining the best people should be your aim—but again, that's something we'll talk about more in the following chapters.

Our View of the Business

The 3 CEOs Formula for successful network marketing subscribes to the power of three. Whether you're building your team, maintaining the team you already have or trying to get up to that next level yourself, there are three separate elements that must be present for success to happen: leadership, action and drive. Each of these is essential, a necessary side of the pyramid. Without one, the other two cannot function, but when all three are merged, they can take you to the top.

Many people get involved with network marketing because they hear that it's easy, quick money and that they can earn millions even though they have little to no experience or education. They get this idea from the advertisements they see: "Earn millions from your home!" "Make thousands a day with your computer!" "Average $20,000 a month today!"

Do these statements look familiar? They should. They represent the public's typical view of network marketing. Too often, people only focus on the wealth that can be earned and not on the real facts—such as the work they'll have to do, or the investments they'll have to make as far as their time, attention and finances. They join up just to get rich quick and when that does not happen right away, they feel cheated or scammed because they in fact fell for something that was not true.

Unfortunately, there are scammers out there. Some people do get taken in (and taken advantage of) by illegal "pyramids"— companies that offer no real product or service in exchange for the initial investment, but still offer the promise of making quick money. Obviously, people who get involved with such things have never heard that if it sounds too good to be true, it probably is.

But that is not how it works for most of us. As The 3 CEOs, we enjoy the money we make through network marketing, but our focus is a little different—a little more dynamic. Instead of just trying to get rich quick, and telling others that they should do the same, we concentrate on creating the best business possible using The 3 CEOs Formula, which combines the essential elements each person needs for long-term success. Once you learn about these elements, how *you* will use them is your choice; each entrepreneur's *personal* formula is different. Throughout this book, you will discover the ingredients necessary to create your personal recipe for success—to come up with your own plan for building a great business based on The 3 CEOs proven methods.

We know, from experience, that a great business doesn't happen overnight; it takes dedication, concentration and time to become something phenomenal. No matter how badly you want it, you cannot force success to happen without putting in the work it requires. Network marketing, we believe, is like building your dream home: If you don't start with a solid foundation, everything you stack on top of it will eventually crumble. You have to ground yourself with a good work ethic and the drive to succeed, using the resources this industry offers—mentors, training, hands-on experience—to become a better person spiritually, mentally, physically and financially. If you have faults in your foundation, such as laziness, procrastination or dishonesty, you have to correct them before success can be yours.

Once your foundation is set, you're ready to start building upward by gathering your associates and putting them to work based on their own skills and strengths. Our view of network marketing centers around the individual, on recognizing each person's talents and helping each person learn and grow as he or she requires. Everyone who enters this industry does so at a different stage of personal development; we don't all come to it knowing everything we have to know. It is only through mentoring and coaching that each of us becomes great, or helps others achieve their full potential.

We have found that in this industry, even with a rock-solid foundation, the program you choose to work with simply becomes the vehicle you use to improve your financial situation. Instead of focusing solely on the monetary rewards, our philosophy embraces the notion that if you value the process of becoming a better person, then everything else, including wealth, can follow.

If you work to properly apply the principles that we discuss in this book, we guarantee you will have the chance to become not just a successful networker, but a better school teacher, minister, nurse, parent, son, daughter or spouse. Network marketing, as we see it, is not just about making yourself rich; it's about making your *life* rich. Don't become a part of this industry simply to become a millionaire. Do it because of who you can become on the journey.

SIDE ONE
LEADERSHIP

Floyd's View

Leaders Build on a Solid Foundation

It takes great leadership to build anything substantial and sustaining. Where would the Disney corporation have ended up without Walt? The Ford Motor Company without Henry? McDonald's without Ray Kroc? They might have been good businesses with decent returns, but chances are, without those dynamic figures at their helms, they would not have grown into the branded empires we know them as today.

Great leaders use their influence to impact others and inspire them to accomplish more. They have the vision to see what's possible when others only see things as they currently are. A great leader uses his or her power of influence to help transform attitudes of doubt and negativity into attitudes of belief and great expectations. A great leader's influence will continue to have a significant impact long after he or she has departed.

In network marketing, your goal is to be that great leader and build your own personal empire through dedication and determination. We've said it before and we'll say it again, both here and in the future: A great business doesn't happen overnight. It takes time to build up your own leadership skills and then use them to recruit and retain the best people out there—to build a strong, solid team that can go the distance. You will have to develop your ability to communicate your ideas, listen effectively and overcome objections as you present your opportunity to others. You'll need to learn to set goals for your business, track your progress and make adjustments along the way. The goal is to be like McDonald's, or Ford, or Disney: to have a company that will last for the rest of your life, and then just keep on going.

The first step you must take toward building this sort of business is putting together a great team, one designed for stability and longevity. Toward this end, you must have stable people on your team—this means individuals who have learned to manage their time and finances, as well as the unexpected challenges that are simply a part of everyday life. Think about it: If half your team is dealing with overwhelming problems at home—with their families, for example, or with debt—how well are they going to perform at work? Distractions in their personal lives can lead to less focus on the tasks they need to do to make your business great, and that is a setback that, often, you cannot afford.

Of course, no one's perfect, and there will come a time when you'll meet someone who seems as though he'd be a great rep— if only he weren't dealing with that messy divorce, or struggling to get himself out of debt. Are people like this worth recruiting? Often, the answer is "yes." Men and women with a little baggage can indeed become your best associates, with just a little guidance and training.

Great leaders develop stability in their team members by setting up proper expectations with them from the very beginning. Here are several key ways to accomplish this:

1. Create a game plan with your new recruits immediately after getting them started, including how much income they expect to earn in the first thirty days, the first six months and the first year. Make sure it's realistic.
2. Find out how much time and effort they're willing to put into their businesses—and how long they're willing to keep it up in order to reach their financial goals.
3. Let new recruits know how much money they will need to invest in their businesses long-term to reach their financial goals.
4. Talk to them about unforeseen obstacles that may arise in their businesses.
5. Discuss things that you have had to overcome in your own business. Talk about how these challenges served to make you a better leader and to make your business stronger.
6. Let your new recruits know that it takes time for any business to become a success, and that their businesses will be no different. It is a three- to five-year process for most people.

Building with integrity—that is, choosing team members based on quality, not quantity—is one of the most critical components of a solid business model. Associates who are invested emotionally in the work they do are more likely to stay with you for the long run, and retention within your organization creates consistency and growth in your income. You need people who are committed to the business just as much as you are, not people who will quit when they aren't rich by the end of the first week.

One thing you should never forget as the leader of your growing empire is that you are not just building a financial vehicle for yourself here—you are actually creating a business made up of people and relationships. In network marketing, you must constantly work to strengthen your relationships with your team members. They must know that you are on their side, and that you sincerely want to see each of them succeed. You have to be genuinely concerned for their well-being and do what you can to foster it; creating a stable environment in which your team can grow and prosper goes a long way toward increasing the profits you earn.

Leaders Don't Make Promises That They Won't Be Able to Keep

How many times have you seen those sensational flyers and advertisements that promise that you can "make $10,000 per month without leaving your home" or "make a six-figure income immediately"? How many times has someone told you, "Just join my team and we'll build a business under you"?

These promises all seem great, but beware of them—and remember that if it sounds too good to be true, it probably is. As an associate, you should never believe anyone's get-rich-quick claims and as a leader, you must never make them to any of your prospective reps, and certainly not to anyone who is already an associate. You just can't guarantee how successful anyone will be. You can't make any promises when it comes to future income.

Nor can you make any vows to spend X amount of time with a person to help them build their business. It sounds like a noble thing to do, especially for someone who is just getting started in network marketing. But there's a difference between training an associate and creating a dependent relationship, and if you set your new reps up to rely on your help for their own success, it could backfire on you later. For instance, if you tell them things like, "When you get started, just give me some names and I'll call them for you" or, "You won't have to worry about doing any presentations—I'll fly in once a month to help you build your team," all you're doing is making more work for yourself that you may not be able to follow through on when the time comes.

Instead of making promises that you won't be able to keep, your job is to get your reps started properly then support them by teaching them how to be self-sufficient in their businesses. Let them know that their objective is to become as independent as they can; make sure they understand that while you are helping them in the beginning, you are preparing them to lead their own future organizations as soon as possible. You can be a great leader for your associates by providing mentoring and advice, but you can't hold their hands forever. Remember, you reap what you sow, and if you've essentially told them that they don't have to do the work, they won't.

Instead, let them know your expectations. Teach them responsibility, and model it to them as well. As the leader, always keep your word concerning commitments you make to help the people on your team. If you're scheduled to do a meeting, show up for it. If you offer incentives such as contests or promotions, honor them. Leaders often lose their credibility by making promises they can't or just don't keep, and if your associates don't believe that you are reliable, they will not do the best work they can for you.

In addition, just as you must ask yourself, "How am I convincing people to join my team?" you must also pay close attention to how your team members are closing their own prospects. What promises are they making to seal the deal? What expectations are they setting up for their new reps—and are those expectations being met? Are your associates overcommitting themselves or making unrealistic promises, ones that just cannot be fulfilled?

If this is how you "roped" your reps into the business, chances are they are using the same techniques, and the cycle of unfulfilled promises is bound to continue—and bound to have a devastating effect on your future income, as well as theirs.

Leaders Don't Create Disappointment by Pushing Unrealistic Timelines

It is important to understand that although network marketing is a unique business, it is in fact a real business and like any other, it takes time to build. Statistics have shown that the average, traditional business takes about three years to break even. Comparatively, even though it is true that network marketing affords anyone the opportunity to make a faster profit with less start-up and overhead costs, statistics also show that for most people to experience significant success, network marketing requires a three- to five-year game plan.

The term "network marketing" even suggests that there is real work involved—it's got that little four-letter word built right into it. One thing you'll hear all of us say, over and over again, is that network marketing is not a get-rich-quick scheme. It's not an illegal pyramid, nor is it a quick hustle. It is a business of technique as well as skill—both of which, if you are new to the business, will take some time for you to acquire and then apply.

As you work your network marketing business, you will begin to learn where and with whom you should be spending the majority of your time. You will learn to make stronger presentations to people simply by doing more of them. You will become a stronger trainer as a result of going to a number of trainings yourself and learning from others who are better than you are—for now.

If you stay plugged in to all the events, trainings, conventions and activities related to your company, you will gradually acquire the skills and techniques that you'll need to have long-term success. The problem is, staying plugged in long-term is a challenge for many people. They start off great, motivated by the excitement of seeing a fantastic presentation by someone who is making a sca-zillion dollars. They enthusiastically attend a few meetings until one day, they realize that they will actually have to do more than just show up at a meeting each week; then the thrill is gone.

Network marketers must work their businesses just like any other entrepreneurs. They need to talk to people about their product or services not just at the company's weekly meetings, but every day. Between the energized meetings and fun-filled conventions, they have to work to market their business and move products or services. If they don't, they'll drift away and be swallowed up by the attrition monster.

Attending all the events and trainings that you can will help you escape this fate. If you stay in the game long enough, you will learn valuable information in trainings and workshops, where leaders will teach you important techniques. You will also benefit from the general conversations that go on at dinner after the weekly meetings, when top leaders discuss their experiences and methods over cheeseburgers, fries and Cokes. Sometimes, these are more powerful than a formal training and if you make it to one, you should consider yourself very fortunate.

If you have been in network marketing for any length of time, you've probably heard of people who have built huge organizations and made thousands and thousands of dollars seemingly overnight. Though this sort of thing is generally considered to be one of the biggest misconceptions in network marketing, it happens on rare occasions. It's just that most overnight sensations come into the industry with either prior successes or significant experience that served to accelerate their growth.

If you are one of those fortunate people, go for it! Use what you know and what you have to break records and head for the top. On the other hand, if you're just a normal person like the rest of us, get ready to pay your dues. Get ready to talk to a great deal of people, do countless home meetings, attend numerous trainings and sponsor a number of people who are willing to do the same.

Three rules to live by in network marketing are:

1. Do not overestimate what you can do in a short period of time. Success in network marketing usually takes longer than most expect it to because, as with anything new, there is a learning curve. Overestimating what you can do can leave you feeling uninspired about small accomplishments that should be celebrated. Each small accomplishment is a stepping-stone toward reaching your overall goal.

2. Do not underestimate what can be achieved in a reasonable amount of time. Because network marketing is built on exponential growth, many people miscalculate what can be achieved long-term. Building a network marketing organization is like having a penny that doubles every day for a year. The compound effects of that are staggering—by the end of it, you'd have well over a million

dollars. In network marketing, the exponential effect of your organization doubling or even tripling can be just as remarkable.

3. Don't compare yourself to other people in the business. People come into network marketing at different levels of understanding about business and the industry itself. You can't measure your success against anyone else's because you may not know his or her entire story.

If you want to be a success in network marketing, the most important things to remember are: Get started, stay consistent, remain teachable, stay focused and never quit. Don't expect to be a millionaire by next year, or to retire by thirty-five. If these things do happen to you, that's great. Enjoy them, because you've probably earned them.

If they don't, then you might want to back up and take a look at your expectations. Are they exceeding your capabilities? Remember, you can only do so much in a day, week or month. Strive to do all you can and be all you can be, but know when to say "when." Pushing yourself and others to do more than is realistically achievable could just end up in failure instead of success.

This concept is never more important than during your first few years in network marketing. While you're waiting for success to kick in, you must remember that it takes time. Many people who are now leaders in the industry in fact earned next to nothing for their first several years, but then took in hundreds of thousands of dollars per year after that. How did this happen? They simply stayed in the game, developed their skills and did the right activities for the first two to three years, including sharing the business opportunity with prospective recruits via home meetings, one-on-one presentations and three-way phone calls. With consistency, they focused on these key activities for building a strong team and creating a solid foundation for exponential growth.

Once you have assembled your team, the next step is to find among them one or two great leaders to generate activity and momentum for everyone else. A couple of successful, motivated individuals can really ignite the entire organization and when that happens, the success multiplies. It grows at lightning speed and before you know it, you—and the people on your team—are getting returns that make up for the previous unproductive years.

Finding these leaders who can propel your team toward success relies on the law of numbers theory, which shows that with a significant number of people generating a large amount of activity, the best will rise to the top. When you're running a sizeable team of talented, skilled associates, all the good work they're doing for you practically assures that you will find your leaders within twelve to twenty-four months. Again, it's just a matter of time.

Unfortunately, some people decide to quit before this can happen, and what a tragedy that is. Many quit because they expected success to come easier or sooner that it normally does. Others just simply drift off course because other things in their life become more of a priority. But there is never a good time to quit—it's always too soon, especially if you've been in the business less than three years. To be honest, anyone who joins a legitimate network marketing company, starts a team and quits before that foundation-setting period is up is absolutely unprofessional and has no business running a business.

It will be most beneficial to you to embrace the idea that success will come, but it will take time. You cannot make it conform to your personal timeline; you must put in all the required work that will bring you to where the success is. And if you can teach this principle to everyone who joins your organization, the payoff will be huge.

Finally, just remember that the next person you meet may make a significant impact on your organization. It could be someone who has the influence to sponsor better people with better skills, and to help your team grow faster and be more productive.

Leaders Don't Drop Their Financial Anchor

Too many people get involved in network marketing with the impression that it will fix all of their existing financial problems. However, it's unrealistic to think that years of improperly handling your finances can be repaired in six months through a network marketing business. Paying off debts and repairing credit takes time, no matter in which industry you work.

For this reason, it makes good business sense to only ask financially stable individuals to join your company. It's important to make sure that every prospect you consider enrolling has a financial vehicle that takes care of their obligations, so you know that they will not be relying on your network marketing venture to support them—at least not in the beginning. Also, make sure that they know not to quit their jobs right away without another steady stream of income in place, no matter how well things seem to be going for them in network marketing.

And the same goes for you. You can and should use your current job to finance your network marketing business and to keep yourself afloat should the business not work out on the first try. Building a network marketing organization can be a very tedious process, and can sometimes even be difficult. Unfortunately, sometimes, what you've built over months can be destroyed overnight, and you have to be willing—and able—to start over.

For example, your organization could be negatively affected by unethical team members. Or, it could be team members who decide to leave your company and devise a scheme to take a large number of your other team members with them to another opportunity. If you've been a good leader, they probably won't be very successful in dismantling your team. But if they are successful, you will have to be prepared and willing to rebuild. Unfortunately, if you are in any sort of financial emergency, this might not be doable, and your dreams of network marketing may remain right where they are—only in your dreams.

Building Leadership Through Mental Toughness

As I mentioned earlier, network marketing is a real business. This means that things can and will go wrong. You will have good days along with challenging ones, and will learn to see the benefit in both.

Any individual who has successfully operated a traditional business will quickly tell you that their success came with an array of challenges, missteps and unexpected obstacles that had to be resolved, and your network marketing business will be no different. If you've already run a traditional company, you have an understanding of the ebb and flow of business, and this can be the fuel that enables you to do better in network marketing than most. You already know that building a business is not easy, but the mental toughness you developed from the process will work in your favor. In network marketing, it's an absolute necessity. Without it, you won't be able to go the distance.

And neither will anyone on your team. Your associates may start out with much enthusiasm and excitement, making big promises and telling you how committed they are to the business. Then, when challenges arise, either personal or within the business, many of these same individuals will go into the witness protection program—meaning you won't be able to find them. Sadly, they may have just decided to quit on you, on themselves and on their dreams.

Sooner or later, you will probably experience a significant purging of your organization because of this phenomenon, and that's okay. Call it evolution in action—those who don't belong will weed themselves out. For most people, it's a natural tendency to walk away from anything that becomes too challenging; just let the quitters quit, and the winners will stay and rise to the top.

When people do leave your business, even though you may have looked at some of them as valuable parts of your team, and regret the loss of their skills, understand that for the time they each spent with you, they served a purpose. They helped you get to a certain level in the business. And when they're gone, you must keep building with your remaining players and continue recruiting to find more leaders who will help you get to the next higher level.

Aside from the usual turnover, every great network marketing company will have times when it is plagued by a host of unexpected problems, such as negative publicity and growing pains. As a leader, your confidence cannot wane during these temporary events. The Bible says a double-minded person is unstable in all their ways (James 1:6), and so you must remain unwaveringly single-minded about all you do, especially in times of crisis. When the going gets tough, you must be mentally tough. You must learn to manage your emotions—and teach your team to do so as well.

The reason for this? Though it's good to feel things like camaraderie and pride in what you do, running a business on emotions such as anger, doubt and fear is a sure formula for disaster. There will be times when you will have to weather the storms of negative publicity, hateful lies, propaganda and unsubstantiated rumors manufactured by uninformed competitors to discredit you and your company. But if you let these things get into your head, you could lose your belief in your business, your confidence, your momentum and, eventually, your entire organization. Remember, you can't necessarily control every negative article or email that may circulate about your business, but there is always one thing you can control: your attitude. Attitude is everything in network marketing!

Building Leadership Through Personal Development

It has been said the fastest and best way to approach chopping down a large tree is to begin by sharpening your ax. In network marketing, which is largely a business of personal development, that is exactly what you must do—first, hone your skills then use them to approach the bigger issues and tasks.

To be successful in network marketing, you must first advance yourself as a leader both at work and at home. Improving your personal skills, such as time management and organization, will make you more valuable in the marketplace, and improving your business acumen will benefit every other area of your life. Becoming an expert in areas such as public speaking, organization, and training and mentoring will undoubtedly lead to increased success in all of your business and social endeavors. These skills can be acquired by attending seminars and workshops about subjects on which you need to improve. Continue to fill your personal library with books and CDs that will allow you to be a lifelong student of personal development.

On the other hand, when you don't have it together on either one side or the other, unfortunately, failure is bound to follow. I'll give you an example: When I owned my advertising agency, I frequently outsourced my print and production work. I specifically remember one gentleman who ran a two-color printing company in Atlanta. Let's just call him Joe, to prevent a lawsuit. His prices were the best in town for small print runs, and I used his services often.

And every time I did, though I saved some money upfront, I ended up paying the difference in the form of headaches and sleepless nights. Joe was always running through his print shop in a panic, trying to fix whatever had just gone miserably wrong. He had an inventory of botched jobs; he never ordered enough paper, could never keep a competent pressman, rarely got jobs out on time and never showed up on time for meetings. In short, he did not have a business—he had work that he created for himself. It was as though he went into his shop every day with a dull ax and hacked away at a giant, dysfunctional tree, grunting with every chop and not feeling too accomplished at the end of the day.

Yet, in all the time that I knew Joe, I never saw him take a course on business, work with a consultant or even ask me how I thought his operation was going. He never stopped to think that maybe his shop was constantly in a state of emergency because he had not first prepared himself to operate a business. He'd never evaluated himself as a businessperson. I'm sure he was a great pressman when he ran the press himself, and I'm sure he had high standards for the work that he produced. But as the owner of this shop, his job was no longer to be a pressman. He was supposed to be an entrepreneur and business owner.

Now, I'm sure that someone had mentored Joe in his day, and taught him how to run printing presses and do all the work that his trade entailed. But who had mentored him when it came to running a business? Probably no one—or, at least, no one who was really qualified to do so. His business was a mess and though he seemed like a nice man, I could only imagine what his personal life was like. Unfortunately, his low prices were not enough to keep his shop afloat, and I had stopped using his services long before he finally closed his doors.

In the ten years that I ran my ad agency, I saw many clients like Joe come and go. They would contract my service to develop their public image on the outside with a fancy logo, a slick brochure and a clever ad campaign. No matter how green they were, I would make them look like they had been in business for decades, even though I knew that they would never see the success they anxiously hoped for. Mostly, this was because they just didn't have good foundations of personal development.

Once, I went to a client's office to present a final package design my agency had created for their hair-care product line. As I presented our work, I had to compete with the television my client had on her desk; my appointment, it seemed, was scheduled for the exact same time as her favorite soap opera. I couldn't believe it—her behavior said so much to me about her personally that I couldn't help thinking that her business would never get anywhere. After that, I made a point of not taking on projects from start-up companies unless I really believed not only in their products, but in their owners as well.

If you are going to operate a network marketing business, make sure that you have the skills, knowledge and information you'll need to be a success in the marketplace—starting with your own personal development. Then, make sure that you have the business acumen—from actual business experience or from the knowledge that comes from mentorship—to operate in this unforgiving arena.

Though you may think that you have what it takes to run a business, do you know what it really takes? Within network marketing, there are principles of business that must be adhered to in order to experience success, and if you violate them, you will be penalized in the form of time and money. The law of sowing and reaping is one of these principles. In network marketing, the sowing is the actual activity that you engage in on a daily basis, such as talking to potential customers about your service or product. The more activity seeds you plant, the more results you will reap. On the other hand, if you are not diligent and you sow very little seeds, you'll pay the price in the form of a meager financial harvest.

Another principle is the law of numbers, which is used in

personal recruiting. All this means is that if you talk to enough people, a ratio of success will appear that will allow you to determine just how many people you will need to talk to in order to sponsor a new recruit. For example, you may find that for every ten people you talk to, you will bring in one recruit. Your ratio will improve as you gain more experience, which you can do by continuing the process of talking to more people.

A good way to find out if you have what it takes is to research the people who are doing what you aspire to, and identify what makes them unique and successful. Are you willing to do what they've done to achieve the same level of success?

One thing to keep in mind is that even those highly successful individuals you strive to emulate were once where you are now. They had to start somewhere, and maybe, when they started out, they knew even less than you do. Everyone comes into a network marketing opportunity at a different level of personal development. Someone who learned how to motivate and lead people in a previous business will get to start further ahead in the journey. Another person who is already a pro at influencing people or speaking with confidence in public gets to go to the front of the success line. Motivated individuals with little or no business skills will find their starting places more toward the back of the crowd—but changing their status and getting ahead is entirely within their control.

Leaders working to build their network marketing teams sometimes become frustrated with these reps who have less experience because their efforts may seem lackluster, slow or uninspired. As a result, some leaders begin to verbally abuse and bully their team, and try to shame them into performing at a higher level. "Why didn't you bring someone to the meeting?" they ask in a badgering tone of voice. "Why is your team not growing faster?" They may even go so far as to say, "You're just not committed like I am."

What leaders who do this don't understand is that many of their team members are working at their maximum level of personal development. Faster results may not be possible for these people—at least, not at the moment. Given time, they will improve, or else they will decide that network marketing is not for them.

If you find yourself with this dilemma and you want faster results, there are only two things you can do: Either go find people who are more personally developed, or provide the leadership and the environment that will allow the people you already have to elevate their levels of personal development. The latter solution will take more time, energy and patience than the first, but often, it's worth it. The loyalty these people will show you for investing so much effort in them will undoubtedly reap rewards for you in the future.

As leaders in network marketing, we face the daily challenges of improving ourselves and teaching others in our businesses to do the same. Personal development is certainly not easy; it is a lifetime journey and often one that we need some help with. So many people, when faced with the opportunity to improve themselves, just don't know where to start.

Most people also don't know, simply, that they don't know. They haven't realized that their personality, their lack of skills, their philosophy and their attitude may be working against them. Some people are not aware of the changes they need to make; some know what they need to do, but don't know how. Others are simply too stubborn to even want to change anything about themselves. After all, don't we all like to think that we're perfect just the way we are?

But we're not—that much is evident. If we were perfect, we would already be successful, wealthy and happy. The first step here is self-discovery—looking inside ourselves, and at our attitudes and actions, and finding what needs to be changed. To become successful, become aware of the behaviors that hold you back, and work to transform them into better, more productive habits. Let's look at this now a little more in-depth.

Self-examination

Personal development is the most important process that you will need to engage in when you become involved in network marketing, and it all starts with self-examination. To achieve your financial goals, you must first embark on a journey of discovery about yourself, to find your strengths and become aware of your weaknesses. This journey will challenge you, make you question how you've operated in the past, and reveal what you need to do to make your life work better in the future.

This period of self-discovery can be an exciting time in your life, and the benefits you reap from it could be even more valuable than the immediate income that many people impatiently look for in network marketing. Without honest self-examination, personal development and growth are just not possible, and so neither are the financial rewards that you want.

If you are not currently achieving the level of success you desire in your business, you need to ask yourself some hard questions about what you have done and what you are currently doing that is preventing you from "being all you can be." Real change doesn't come as a result of going to a seminar or hearing a motivational speech. We begin to get results in our lives when we start to change the way we think about things, and when we change the way we think, we change the way we do.

As an example, let me tell you about a gentleman I once helped out who was holding a business presentation in his home. When he greeted his guests at the door, he wore a badly wrinkled shirt and had shower shoes on his feet—and that's not even mentioning his demeanor, which was nonchalant and unenthusiastic. He had been drinking wine with some of the early-arrival guests, and they had gotten pretty relaxed (read: drunk) in the process. This was standard operating procedure for him.

Obviously, that business presentation did not go very well and, honestly, neither did any other endeavor this man pursued because he lacked the motivation to look inside himself and see what he was doing wrong. I knew, however, that until he changed his mind about how to conduct his business, he would never change the way he behaved, and he would never move to a higher level of success.

In order to change the way you act, you have to change your thinking. In order to change your thinking, you must change the information you've been receiving from the environment, ideas, concepts and people surrounding you. All of these factors determine how we do things, and how we do things determines how successful we become. Perhaps the gentleman in the above scenario never had a good friend or associate pull him aside and tell him just what kind of impression he was making on potential prospects. If someone had, he might have seen the error of his ways, worked harder on improving his presentation and made more money in the long run.

If you need to change your thinking, start by changing your environment and your circle of influence. Instead of hanging around the same old friends who hold dead-end jobs and have no aspirations in life, surround yourself with great business leaders. Read what they read, go where they go, and make the type of decisions that they make, and you will be on your way toward becoming the next great business leader yourself.

My Personal Development Journey

I have gone to the top of several network marketing companies in less than eight months each.

Wait, let me rephrase that: It was eight months after several years of hard work, personal development and self-examination.

With my first network marketing opportunity, it took me three years to get to that point. I went to every weekly meeting, every weekly training session and every convention I could, and dedicated every spare moment I had to learning, developing and building. In that three-year time period, I would estimate that I earned a total of less than $5,000.

Most people would see that as a complete waste of time. Even I wondered if I was spending so much valuable time chasing a pipe dream. However, I later came to realize that even though my income was temporarily low, I was, in reality, worth millions. Thanks to those early years that I spent developing myself and my skills, I was becoming more than I had ever been, and was preparing myself to take in the millions of dollars I have since earned in the network marketing industry.

In those days, every meeting, phone conference and presentation that I attended was like a financial deposit into my future. Every lesson I learned and every skill I developed brought me that much closer to my financial goals. And, with each network marketing opportunity that presented itself to me, I was able to make larger and larger withdrawals from my personal development bank and use them to invest in my future wealth.

If you were to ask me today which is more valuable, the millions I have earned or the personal development journey that got me to the income, I would tell you without hesitation that it's the journey. Why? Because money comes and goes, but the process of acquiring knowledge and then applying it can transform you into someone who can consistently make success happen.

I can still remember the beginning of my personal development journey. I had been running a home-based advertising and graphic design studio for a couple of years. I had acquired a few good clients and was earning some income, but things were not going as well as I desired them to. One evening, I decided to go to a networking event with the hope of meeting some potential clients.

It was there where I met a lady named Lorna, who was working with a personal development company that specialized in leadership development.

After a short discussion with her about my business, she enthusiastically recommended that I consider taking a look at what her company could offer to a small business owner like myself, and gave me a sample video to watch. I politely accepted her video, took it home and placed it in the back of a drawer in my desk. Not knowing that it would serve as the catalyst for the beginning of a life-long process of personal development, it remained in my desk drawer for months.

And then, one day, I received a fax from Lorna inviting me to attend a seminar and learn more about the personal development company for which she worked. Later on, while working late into the night—and almost right into the next morning—I remembered the videotape she'd given me. I went to my desk, opened the drawer and searched through piles of business junk until I finally retrieved the video. I dusted it off, popped it into the player and watched with utter amazement the information, concepts and ideas that would change my life forever.

In the video, a gentleman spoke and wrote information down on a white board, and he seemed to be talking directly to me. He was saying things like, "Income seldom exceeds personal development" and, "What you become directly influences what you get."

That man's name was Jim Rohn, and he was one of Americas most-recognized business philosophers. He went on to say, "Don't become a victim of yourself. Forget about the thief waiting in the alley. What about the thief in your mind?" This was powerful for me. I could not wait to learn more not only from Jim, but from other great business trainers and authors who had been waiting for me to come to class. Someone once said, "When the student is ready the teacher will appear," and that was true—I was ready, and there they were.

Over the next few years, I was like a sponge, absorbing as much personal development information as I could. I purchase books and CDs, and paid hundreds of dollars to attend seminars held by some of the top business speakers and trainers in the world. I then began to apply the concepts, skills and ideas that I acquired in my business, and I saw incredible results. Using my newfound business skills, I went on to build a successful, brick-and-mortar advertising agency with better clients and better-paying projects. Rather than choosing to invest money and time into my business, I first made the investment of working on myself, and the benefits I gained from that were enormous.

Over the years, I have been blessed to experience success in many different business arenas. I have worked in corporate America, started home-based businesses, run network marketing businesses and even formed and operated traditional, brick-and-mortar companies. Through these experiences, I have discovered that while each of these areas has distinct characteristics, they all require someone at the helm who possesses the necessary leadership skills and business acumen to operate them successfully, including goal-setting, organization, time management and people skills. These qualities are transferable to any business arena, and if mastered, can make you the absolute best in your industry.

I often talk about the concept of working to brand yourself as an intellectual property, which is defined as something that comes from the work of your own mind. What this means is that you can change yourself; you can develop into whomever and whatever you want to be. Today, I continue to use personal development to make myself more valuable in the marketplace, and I continue to apply my business and leadership skills to create documentation and a proven track record of success. Documentation is a key ingredient that has allowed great speakers, authors and leaders to brand themselves as experts and market their expertise in the form of books, CDs and speaking careers.

Spencer's View

Leadership Through Personal Development

Network marketing is the single greatest industry for leadership development and self-discovery. It will expose every character flaw and illuminate every gift that you have. If you are a procrastinator, inherently lazy or dishonest, if you have a poor work ethic and tend to cut corners in life, or if you have a small circle of influence, network marketing will expose it. If you have a knack for leadership, the ability to motivate people and a head full of business experience, network marketing will bring those qualities out as well. Either way, the "true you" will be revealed.

Most of us look at ourselves subjectively, not objectively. This means that we often have an impression of ourselves that differs dramatically from the opinions of those around us. Granted, nobody is perfect; we all have areas upon which we can improve. The key is recognizing and accepting that we all have room to grow, and that self-discovery will help you improve in the areas of your life that need more development and ultimately help you become a better leader.

In this first section, as we look at the first side of The 3 CEOs Formula's pyramid, I'm going to break the concept of leadership development down into three steps: admission, awareness and application. Each of these steps is a vital milestone that will help you realize your full potential as a leader in your business, on your job and in your life.

Step One: Admission

The road to recovery, they say, begins with admitting that you have a problem. While we're not talking about addictions here, there is an aspect of recovery involved in the self-examination process you must undergo when building a network marketing business. To get away from your current unproductive habits and move on to more meaningful and significant work, you must first know that you have a problem, and that you need help to remedy it. Are you lazy? Admit it. Scared of making mistakes? Admit that, too. Whatever it is that's holding you back, you have to own it—and then, you have to let it go.

Unfortunately, our biggest deterrent to admission is always pride. Overinflated egos have caused so many people to miss great opportunities in life, just because they were too proud to admit that they were not working to the best of their ability, or not taking full advantage of their skills, or doing something in a way that was less than optimal.

Pride can unnecessarily hold you back from achieving greatness because it creates an unwillingness to look at an opportunity from another person's perspective and see that maybe your own way is not the best way. Pride precludes a degreed professional from even looking at a network marketing business opportunity because he thinks it is "beneath" him. Pride makes a man prohibit his wife from fully engaging in the business for fear that she will make more money than he does. Pride causes a wife to withhold support from her husband because she dislikes the attention that all his success brings upon him. Pride, if ill-applied, can be a bad thing.

In our journey as The 3 CEOs, we have encountered numerous people who entered the networking business with much fanfare. They came on with all of these great assertions about how many people they knew, how many they were going to recruit, how fast they were going to do it and how many records they would break in the process. But once they got started and began to see how difficult this business really is, that same pride would not allow them to admit that they couldn't handle it, and that they needed help. It seemed to be easier for them to make excuses for their poor performance and quit the business altogether than face the embarrassment of accepting that their flaws had been exposed by the difficult nature of the industry.

Step Two: Awareness

If you can successfully conquer step one, and admit that you have a problem that needs to be addressed, then you are ready for the second step in leadership development: becoming aware of resources that can help you improve your deficiencies.

One resource that you should definitely look into is self-improvement books and CDs. Floyd Williams, my partner and mentor, is a big advocate of them; he has audio books in his house, in his attaché and all over his car. Self-improvement seems to always be on his mind, and that reveals itself in his life and in his work.

Some of the titles we suggest you check out include:

- *The Slight Edge: Secret to a Successful Life* by Jeff Olsen (Momentum Media, 2005)
- *Why We Want You to Be Rich: Two Men, One Message* by Donald J. Trump and Robert T. Kiyosaki (Rich Press, 2006)
- *Rich Dad, Poor Dad* by Robert T. Kiyosaki and Sharon L. Lechter (Warner Books, 2000)
- *Who Moved My Cheese? An Amazing Way to Deal with Change in Your Work and in Your Life* by Spencer Johnson and Kenneth Blanchard (G. P. Putnam's Sons, 1998)

However, my ultimate resource for personal and leadership development is the Bible and whether you are a Christian or not, I recommend it highly. Floyd and I have attended church together for several years, and we talk about biblical principles all the time. We have seen them at work in our own lives and the lives of many people we know.

Perhaps one of the biggest lessons I've learned from the Bible is that in life, there are certain inescapable principles that we simply cannot ignore; they are absolutes, and violating them, just like breaking the law, has consequences. Here, I've chosen three fundamental biblical principles to discuss with you that I think will help you become a better, more successful person both in business and in life.

The first principle is often known as the "law of labor." In II Thessalonians 3:10, we read, "For even when we were with you, this we commanded you, that if any would not work, neither should he eat." This means that you are rewarded according to the effort that you exert. If you don't do the work, you should not expect to reap the benefits.

Great business leaders understand this principle and strive to apply it in their daily lives because they know they'll never get to be the next Donald Trump or Bill Gates without putting some work into it. They know that they must wake up each morning with a game plan for the day and make every effort to execute each task on their list. They also know that even when they're at the top of their games, running companies that are leaders in their industry, they must continue putting forth that effort every day because if they don't, they will not earn whatever reward comes next.

Great leaders in networking operate just the same. Every day, they do the small things their businesses require—three-way calls, attending meetings and conventions, and conducting team trainings—with the knowledge that over time, these things will mean the difference between success and failure.

People often wonder why they have not accomplished more in their lives and often it can be attributed to the lack of real work that they exert. Activity is often mistaken for productivity; in other words, some people *look* busy, but really aren't doing much of substance. You may know people who are constantly making phone calls, answering emails and handing out business cards, but that doesn't mean that they're bringing in prospects—or paying customers.

To illustrate this point, let's look at a former member of our organization who hailed from Milwaukee, Wisconsin. Now, when she worked with us, she lived hundreds of miles away from Milwaukee, but periodically traveled there to work on building her team. She conducted meeting after meeting in the city, she told us, in an effort to find new reps and prospects.

I called this woman often, just to see how her recruiting efforts were going. Her response was always positive and optimistic, even though the company reports clearly showed her lack of progress. Over several months and quite a few trips to Milwaukee, only two or three people had joined her team.

Eventually, I had to advise her to look into cultivating another market because while she was certainly *active* with all those trips and meetings, she was not *productive*.

Unfortunately, she refused to quit because Milwaukee was her hometown, and she just wasn't ready to leave it behind. However, months later, she came back to me and admitted that her excursions there *had* been a waste of time and money. She had been guilty of making emotional decisions regarding her business instead of focusing on what would really get her ahead.

She was also guilty of being ineffective and inefficient, two qualities that can sabotage one's leadership development. A lack of efficiency in your business can lead to a waste of time and money, but mastering efficiency as a skill will produce exponentially higher returns throughout your organization.

A complementing scripture to the law of labor principle is found in Ecclesiastes 9:10, which states, "Whatsoever thy hand findeth to do, do it with all thy might." In other words, whatever you decide to do in life, do it to the best of your abilities. Whenever you take on a task—from running a meeting to recruiting a prospect to training new team members—you should attack it with all the skill you have. Remember that leaders want the best for themselves and others, and understand that mediocre efforts produce mediocre results.

Your own business' success or failure will often be determined by the pride you take in making it the best that you can, and this goes for any endeavor you pursue in life. Always make it tough for anyone else to live up to the standard that you set. If you decide to become a schoolteacher, don't settle for being an average instructor—try to become the teacher your students will never forget. If you work as a nurse or other medical professional, give your patients the quality of service and care that leaves them with a positive memory of what could have otherwise been a difficult experience.

Becoming successful in any venture demands persistence. You must give whatever you're doing your best effort all the time. As a leader, you have to honestly ask yourself, "Am I really giving 100 percent to this opportunity? Am I trying my best to be my best?"

When I was growing up, my father would often tell my brothers and me, "I don't care what you end up doing in life as long as it's honest. If you're a ditch-digger, be the best ditch-digger in town!" and that's advice that I took to heart.

Before we became involved full-time in network marketing, Floyd, Donald and I worked very, very hard in our respective careers. We each had aspirations of being the best at what we did, and we worked every day to make that happen.

Once we got into network marketing, we did not want to build a mediocre team; we wanted to build one of the best ever! So, we simply transferred the drive and persistence we had in our other jobs into a different vehicle, and were rewarded financially for doing so.

I think that sometimes people grossly underestimate how hard it is to become financially free through network marketing.

It's not just something that happens because you want it to; as the scripture states, we worked our networking business "with all our might," often to the point of exhaustion. We put in hundreds of sleepless nights, thousands of phone presentations and personal meetings, and millions of miles driving in rental cars to build a financial empire that will last for generations, long after we are gone. Has it been worth it? Absolutely. None of us would change one minute of what we've done.

The second principle is known as the law of sowing and reaping. Galatians 6:7-9 states, "Be not deceived; God is not mocked: for whatsoever a man soweth, that shall he also reap... And let us not be weary in well doing; for in due season we shall reap, if we faint not." I could write an entire book on this principle!

I'm not much of a farmer, but I understand one simple concept: If you plant watermelon seeds, you can expect watermelons to grow. However, there is some work that has to be done first—the soil must be prepared, the earth must be tilled and fertilized, and there must be ample amounts of sun and water. You can't simply throw the seeds on the ground, neglect them and then expect them to miraculously produce a bountiful harvest.

I know that this sounds like common sense, but you'd be surprised at some people's expectations. Many think that they can simply invest in a new business, work it for a little while, then sit back and wait for the postal service to deliver thousands of dollars worth of checks to their doorsteps. Of course, this is wrong. There is no "sitting back" in business—not if you want yours to grow. You must do something with your business every day and develop yourself as a leader; you can't take a week off here and a month off there and expect your business to be productive in your absence. What you need to do is invest your time in it diligently, and work and work and work. Then, when harvest time comes, it will be bountiful.

Further, you will reap according to the measure with which

you sow. If you plant a lot of "seeds," you can expect a larger harvest than a person who does not. Network marketing is a numbers game and in your business, the more qualified people you talk to everyday, the more people you can expect to join your organization.

During the sowing process, good leaders anticipate and prepare for the "storms" that may affect their productivity. In Georgia, beginning in 2005, a severe drought affected the livelihood of farmers and the entire agricultural industry throughout the Southeast. This drought cost the agricultural industry millions of dollars. Some farmers who had never prepared for catastrophe were devastated, and essentially lost everything. Then there were others who, in anticipation of a market downturn, had planned months and years ahead, stockpiling resources and managing their money so they could survive during the storm. They understood that there would be years or "cycles" when growing conditions would not always be ideal because of drought, flood, pestilence or disease. The farmers who prepared themselves in anticipation of the "storm" were the ones who ultimately made it.

My Personal Development Journey

Lord knows I've had my share of "storms." As I went through grade school, college and law school, I excelled in practically everything, both academically and athletically. I won everything to which I set my mind; I was a perennial student council president and garnered numerous honors and awards. When I was in the eighth grade, AutoCad sponsored a national competition to promote a line of computer-aided design software it had just developed. They asked students around the country to design their best rendition of a number two pencil, and there were thousands of entries. I came in second place and won a scholarship, plus $12,000 worth of AutoCad software for my school.

During my senior year of high school, I applied for one of the most competitive and prestigious college scholarships in America, from the Coca-Cola Scholars Foundation. Each year, more than 100,000 of the country's best students applied for the award; only fifty were selected to receive a four-year, $20,000 scholarship to the school of their choice.

After surviving an initial essay screening, I was flown to Atlanta with 150 other semi-finalists and subjected to an interview process with four of America's most accomplished leaders in business and education. Two weeks later, I was chosen as one of the fifty finalists!

In all, I had accumulated more than $300,000 in scholarship offers before graduating from high school. After graduation, I continued to excel in college at Georgia Tech. While there, I developed a new concept for a toothpick that also served as a unique marketing tool for restaurants. I named it Promopick and at the age of twenty-three, was awarded a patent for the idea.

I then went on to develop a basketball goal for the visually impaired called Sonaball (a combination of "sonar" and "ball"). I would often leave my marketing class at Tech, put on my one good suit, and visit the Academy for the Visually Impaired to conduct demonstrations and refine the product.

Things seemed to be going very well for quite a while, but the storm clouds eventually began to roll in for me. By the time I'd graduated from law school, I had developed a pretty healthy amount of self-confidence; you might even say that I was arrogant. I was pretty good at everything I did—though, unfortunately, I knew it. I was a top-notch graduate, I had just married Tonya, my gorgeous college sweetheart, and I was making some pretty good money. I was the only minority in my graduating class to have a job waiting for me after graduation—all I had to do was pass this silly little test called the bar exam.

No problem, I thought. I'd always done okay on standardized tests; I'd performed above average on the SAT and LSAT, though I hadn't blown those tests out of the water as I'd expected to. But that was okay—I was confident that I could ace the bar exam regardless of past performance. When I took the exam, I felt really good. There were no "curve balls," and I was familiar with all of the subject matter. After the test, when I went back to the firm where I worked, I was congratulated by my fellow associates and by the partners for completing this rite of passage.

The bar exam results came in about six weeks later. That day, my phone rang off the hook with friends calling in from around the country, letting me know that they had passed and congratulating me—even though I had not yet checked my mail and did not know my results. When I finally got home that evening, all ready to enjoy a celebratory dinner with my wife, I got the mail and tore open my letter. To this day, the only words I remember are "We regret to inform you..."

I just about fainted. I curled up on the bed, barely mustering the strength to call Tonya and say, "I need you to come home." I felt like I'd been struck by a Mack truck. I thought that this couldn't be happening to me.

But the next day, I had a little more perspective. *Get over it*, I told myself. *Just study harder this time, and retake the stupid test.* And that was what I did, even though I was under a lot of stress both from my job at the law firm and from myself.

When the day came to take the bar exam for a second time, I was so embarrassed as I walked down the aisle. Why? Because now I was taking the test with people who had graduated *after* me. I felt like a flunky, and I guess that, technically, I was. But I stuck with it and took the test.

And I failed again. Strike two.

I figured that there must have been some hidden conspiracy

against me within the state of Georgia. Or, maybe I had inadvertently upset one of my professors, and they were now exacting their revenge. Maybe this was an MTV show and I was being "Punk'd"!

Nope—no cameras, no gotcha! So I went on to study for the exam a third time. By the time I took the crazy test again, the stress had become so intense that I'd begun to develop constant, shooting pains in the back of my neck and shoulders—a condition that just got worse when I found out that I'd failed the bar exam again. Strike three, and I was out.

To this day, one of the most embarrassing and depressing moments of my life was having to walk from my car to the twenty-story building where my office was located, ride the elevator to the top floor and essentially draft a letter of resignation to the firm that had hired me with so much hope and promise. Being the only minority, I felt an even deeper sense of failure as I felt a greater obligation to be an example to whoever might have been following in my footsteps.

During my time with the firm, I had built a pretty solid practice representing professional athletes, and when I left, I decided to pursue this full-time. I also developed a legal recruiting company, and was making between $30,000 and $50,000 per month. I felt like I was on the road to recovery.

Then, the events of September 11, 2001, occurred. I will never forget that day. I sat in front of the television in horror, watching in real time the second attack on the World Trade Center in New York. I watched as the two iconic towers collapsed to the ground, instantly killing thousands of people. I remember the simultaneous reports from Washington, D.C., where similar attacks were occurring on the Pentagon.

That morning, I received a call from D.C., from my top client in the recruiting business. She let me know that all interviews had been cancelled due to "some explosion" in the area. I had been set to make $12,000 from that client that day but after that phone call, I never heard from them again.

I had a difficult time recovering from the emotional trauma of witnessing the devastation that occurred on 9/11, and so did my business. From that day forward, things grew worse and worse for us financially. For months, I hoped that the situation would improve, but the economy continued to take a turn for the worst in the post-9/11 era. My savings began to dwindle to almost nothing.

Then, I had a great idea. Though the "dot coms" were tanking on the NASDAQ, I realized that two trends were emerging in the high-tech sector: high-speed Internet and streaming video. In response to this, I developed a line of products called Political Views, which allowed politicians, who typically spend millions of dollars on media campaigns, to stream their personal messages and campaign commercials to hundreds of thousands of potential constituents via the Internet and email. This method came in at a fraction of the cost when compared to "paper" promotions, which involved lots of labor and postage; it was also a much more personal way to introduce candidates to voters who were unfamiliar with their platforms. In addition, I could provide the politician with valuable demographic information on those who actually opened and watched their presentations.

Using the same concept, I developed a product called Prep Promotions, which high school students around the country could use to highlight clips of their athletic accomplishments. I amassed a database of more than 20,000 email addresses of colleges and universities to which the students could send their videos; with my product, high school athletes from small areas could get scholarship consideration from colleges that may never have heard of them otherwise. And because the entire package was delivered via email, it was easy for coaches to review and forward the videos, and to correspond with the students—much more so than when dealing with bulky videotapes and CDs. I later developed a similar product for aspiring professional athletes, called Pro Promotions.

I must say, I think that this predecessor of the YouTube concept was brilliant. The only thing I needed to take it to the big-time was money—remember, I was broke. By this time, my son, Brandon, had been born and I was doing whatever I could to put food on the table. I did consulting work and odd jobs here and there—virtually anything to keep from going back to work in corporate America.

And all the while, I was meeting with venture capitalist groups and wealthy people I knew, trying to secure funding for my new company. I just needed somebody to believe in me. But the more time that passed, the deeper in debt I became. Each week, my wife and I had to choose whether to attend the morning or evening church service because we did not have the gas money for both. One month, I even had to pawn a customized Rolex just to pay for daycare. That hurt, but I was realistic enough with myself to see the hypocrisy of wearing a $7,000 watch and not being able to keep up with my bills. Fortunately, I've never been too emotionally attached to material things.

Things continued to worsen until I had to ask my parents for money. I vividly remember them giving me, without question, their entire income tax return for that year. Keep in mind that my father, a small-town minister, and my mom, a retired schoolteacher, had six kids together—talk about sacrifice! When they agreed to help me out, I continued to be prayerful, as what they gave me was just enough to allow us to catch up and secure some breathing room.

I was—and am—the most optimistic person in the world. Even in such a dire situation, each day, I woke up knowing that *this* would be the day the phone would ring and I would get the answer I had been waiting for. *This* would be the day when someone was willing to fund my company. This day just could not come soon enough.

The money Mom and Dad had loaned me soon ran out and again, I had to borrow—this time, from my in-laws. It doesn't get much lower than that. I remember my mom coming up for a visit one weekend and taking me shopping at SuperTarget and Sam's Club, where she bought us about $200 worth of groceries. I felt like a king! I had lost so much weight during that time that seeing all of the good food in those shopping baskets just about brought tears to my eyes!

But buying us food was not the only thing on my mother's mind that day. Before we'd left, she'd told me to put on some nice clothes. I'd thought it a little strange to dress up for a shopping trip, but since she was paying, who was I to complain? Turned out that while we were at SuperTarget and Sam's Club, she strongly suggested that I fill out applications for employment—and I did. However, I applied for night stocking positions so that just in case I was hired, nobody I knew would happen to see me wearing a red apron and a name badge saying, "Hi, my name is Spencer!"

As I tried to weather this storm, though I didn't entirely realize it at the time, God was teaching me humility—another essential component of leadership development. Would I be humble enough to consider accepting employment at stores where I was clearly overqualified? Or would my pride preclude me from supporting my family properly? Only time would tell.

Two weeks after I filled out those applications, I had one last chance to get funding for my company. Everyone, so far, had told me "no." I just needed one "yes." My partner and I were both *literally* down to our last dimes even though, ironically, we represented clients who were worth millions of dollars.

We had one client to whom we thought IP Promotions might appeal. At the time, he was pitching in Florida for spring training. We talked to him over the phone and told him about the investment we were looking for, and he sounded excited. He told us to come on down to discuss the details in person.

Between the two of us, we had just enough gas money to get to Orlando, Florida, though we had no idea how we would get back home. We decided to save money by sleeping at my parents' home in a southern Georgia town called Valdosta but other than that, we were kind of playing it by ear. As we set out on the trip, I made up in my mind that if this deal did not work out, I would forget about the whole idea and get a "real job."

This was where God was testing my faith. We were driving to Florida with no money, no food and no plan for what would happen if this superstar baseball player said "no." From the outside, no one could tell how badly we were doing—we were riding in my partner's black Infinity sedan, and I had on one of my DW Designs, custom-tailored suits—but we were so hungry. Each time we passed a Waffle House or Cracker Barrel restaurant on Interstate 75, my eyes would just fill with tears. My partner's hands started looking like little chicken fingers on the steering wheel!

We finally arrived at Disney's Wide World of Sports Complex, where our client was pitching that day. Luckily, he had arranged for us to get in free. We were still so hungry, and all the kids—they were everywhere—seemed to be taunting us with their ice cream cones and hot dogs.

We sat in the stands and watched our client pitch for a while, waiting for our chance to talk to him. As we waited, we got a phone call from the wife of another client—a professional golfer who owed us an installment of $800 on a previous contract. He had been stalling the payment for weeks. Now, his wife was saying that just a few moments earlier, she had wired the $800 to my checking account! I must have knocked down about ten kids as I ran to the nearest ATM to check, and sure enough, the money was there. *See how good God is?* I thought. *He may not be there when you want Him, but He's always right on time!*

Back in the stands, tears streamed down my face as my partner and I bit into the most succulent hot dogs I think we had ever tasted!

The game finally ended, and our client took us out to dinner. We proposed our idea to him, and he fell in love with it! He immediately called his financial planner and made arrangements to personally fund our company—including putting both my partner and me on yearly salaries that were more than my initial salary at the law firm. Even though this same client stole my company from me with his team of attorneys years later, which is a story for another book, the point here is that God can bring you out of any trial if you put all of your trust in Him and manage to weather the storm.

Many of you may be going through a "storm" as you read this. Anything that hinders your progress can be a storm. Yours might be illness, a bad relationship, financial distress, depression or low self-esteem. But surviving the storm depends on you, your faith and your level of preparation to weather whatever comes your way.

I encourage you to remember this: You are better than your current situation. Whatever you are going through right now is most likely not permanent, and you do have the power to change it. Your journey in leadership development is going to be filled with various tests and trials, but you must remain focused on your goals and your "why"—your reason for wanting to become financially free. It has been said that a man can never become a great captain by navigating smooth waters, and the same concept applies here. It's not how many times you get knocked down in life—it's how many times you get back up.

While you're building your business, "life" is going to happen, so prepare for it now. The quicker you can rebound from a situation, the quicker you can get back in the game. Business can be very cruel, and the competition can and will use your moment of grief, pain or despair as an opportunity to take you out of business. You have to do like the popular deodorant commercial says: "Never let 'em see you sweat." In business, this means learning how to suffer hardships and keep on working, without your competitors—or even your team—ever knowing that you had a problem at all.

Listen, Learn and Lead

Turning again to the principle of sowing and reaping, let's look at how it also applies to ethics. The network marketing industry's reputation has been damaged somewhat by its image of being "ethically challenged." Unfortunately, Floyd, Donald and I have witnessed this first-hand as we have built our organizations around the world.

While building your own business, one thing you must understand is that what goes around comes around. A farmer who plants defective seeds can expect a defective harvest, and if you choose to be dishonest with guests, "steal" prospects, create schemes to defraud companies by manipulating the compensation plan, or a host of other ethical violations, they will ultimately come back to you, and the repercussions are simply not worth it.

J. Lloyd "Coach" Tomer, one of the great founders of a leading online travel company, always says, "If it ain't right, don't do it and if it ain't true, don't say it." Great leaders understand that people watch every move that they make—both good and bad. I sleep well each night knowing that I have been truthful and honest in building my business, and I want to teach those same qualities to my team. If your organization has been built on a faulty premise, it may work for a short while, but in the long run, it will crumble beneath you. There's no way to escape this. Why?

Because you have violated the principle and now must reap the consequences.

The latter part of Galatians 6:9 reads, "...for in due season we shall reap, if we faint not." This speaks to the concept of endurance. Many people won't make it to the finish line simply because they will quit. I once worked with a young man from North Carolina who was following The 3 CEOs system to the letter. He was recruiting up, doing three-way calls and working his business every day. We worked together at a feverish pace for about two weeks—but with no results.

Late one night, he called me, frustrated, and said, "Mr. Iverson, I've done everything you've asked me to and I see that this opportunity just isn't going to work for me. I'll talk it over with my wife, but I think we're going to quit."

This young man was a dynamic leader, and I would have been sad to see him go. Fortunately, the day after we had that conversation, five people joined his business and gave him reason to stay! What he'd failed to realize was that he had planted some good "seeds" in the days and weeks before then, and the seeds just needed some time to germinate. If he'd quit, he never would have seen the results of his hard work; he would have missed the event that eventually led him to earn thousands of dollars. Thomas Edison once said, "Many of life's failures are people who did not realize how close they were to success when they gave up," and it's amazing how true those words really are.

The third and final principle we'll look at in relation to successful network marketing is the law of instruction. Proverbs 1:5 and 8 state, "A wise man will hear, and will increase learning; and a man of understanding shall attain unto wise counsels... My son, hear the instruction of thy father, and forsake not the law of thy mother." This means that if you're smart, you'll heed the words of your instructors and mentors, and respect their knowledge based on the success that they have already achieved.

Basically, it says that in order to be a good leader, you must first be a good follower.

The easiest way to become successful is to find someone who already is, and ask him or her to teach you how it's done. Understand the importance of seeking wise counsel, and be open to receiving instructions. Also, realize that not everyone who claims to be successful actually is. There are many "experts" out there who are nothing more than opportunists, preying on the frailties of human nature to promote their own causes and agendas.

Recognize as well that not everyone is qualified to give advice. Don't listen to just anyone; instead, try to learn from someone who has navigated the treacherous waters of business ownership and entrepreneurship and emerged victorious. People who have successfully navigated storms have learned lessons and gained experience from which they can teach and what they have to say will undoubtedly prove to be the most valuable instruction you can receive.

One thing I want you to notice is the order of the instructions in Proverbs 1:5. A wise person will first *hear* and then *increase learning*. Too often, people don't want to listen first—they think they already have all the answers. But critical listening is a skill, and one that we all must cultivate if we want to get anywhere in business, and in life. I had to learn how to listen critically while I was in law school because I could not effectively represent my clients if I did not first listen to their presentations of the facts and determine the issues relevant to their cases. Only after listening to this information could I begin to determine whether or not a legitimate claim existed.

When I'm around Floyd and Don, I listen. These two are brilliant businessmen with strengths in areas where I am particularly weak, and the more I listen to them, the more I learn. Likewise, in your leadership development efforts, make it a habit to increase your knowledge about something each month just by listening to someone else. Learn more about what it takes to run a business. Learn more about your industry and the trends that affect it. Learn more about your strengths and weaknesses, and what tactics you can utilize to improve the areas you need to. In so doing, you will learn more about becoming a better you.

Be the Leading Man

While out on a road trip, Donald and I were talking about the similarities that existed between Floyd, himself and me. Don said that he had been listening to Floyd and me talk with and train our teams over the years and had come to realize that each of us was heavily influenced by the instructions of our fathers, to paraphrase Proverbs 1:8. Each of us was raised with a mom and a dad at home, with all of the family and spiritual benefits that came from growing up in such an environment.

While the importance of women and mothers is well-documented and rightfully so, there has been a significant and dramatic decline in the number of men who are taking care of their children, stepping up and being the leaders and role models that their families deserve. Where are our dads? For children, not having a strong father-figure present in their lives can lead to some depressing outcomes. When a father is not present, it increases the likelihood of:

- The children becoming addicted to alcohol and drugs (Deane Scott Berman, "Risk Factors Leading to Adolescent Substance Abuse," *Adolescence* 30, 1995: 201-206).
- The family living in a state of poverty because Mom has to be the sole provider for the kids (U.S. Department of Health and

Human Services, National Center for Health Statistics, Survey on Child Health, Washington, D.C., 1993).

- Earlier sexual activity in children, which often leads to teen pregnancy (U.S. General Accounting Office, "Families on Welfare: Teenage Mothers Least Likely to Become Self-Sufficient," U.S. Government Printing Office, Washington, D.C., May 1994).

- Risk of suicide due to issues of low self-esteem and depression (U.S. Department of Health and Human Services, National Center for Health Statistics, Survey on Child Health, Washington, D.C., 1993).

- Emotional and behavioral problems at school; children of fatherless homes are less likely to graduate from high school and are more likely to go to prison (G.D. Sandefur [et al], "The Effects of Parental Marital Status...Social Forces," September 1992; D. Cornell [et al], "Behavioral Sciences and the Law," 5, 1987 and N. Davidson, "Life Without Father," *Policy Review*, 1990).

It is impossible to adhere to the principles found in Proverbs if a father is not around to give instruction. As The 3 CEOs, we feel that it is time for men to be men and accept the God-given roles assigned to them.

I thank God everyday for blessing me with my beautiful son and daughter, Brandon and Hayley. I challenge myself to be a "professional dad"—one who is always around, much like mine was for me while I was growing up. I remember how, when I was a senior in high school, I was involved in just about everything and on one particular day, I had a conflict between two events. I was the president of one of the school's clubs and we had advanced to the state finals of a competition that was being held somewhere in southern Georgia. On the same day, in another city later in the afternoon, I had my very first track meet. I know that my dad was particularly happy about this one because he had been a world-class sprinter in college, and I had just been chosen to be the anchor leg for our track team's 4X100 relay team.

As busy as my dad was, he drove me all the way to the southern Georgia town where my first event was being held, and then raced me across the state to the track meet. And, though he had a meeting to attend later that evening, he stayed to see me run my first race.

As the starting gun sounded, I was shaking like a leaf because there were so many people at this meet, and the 4x100 was typically the premier event at a track and field event. My best friend, Chris Hart, ran the first leg; he took off like he'd been shot out of a cannon. We had a small lead going into the second exchange, and I was able to see the whole race unfold as I stood on my mark in turn four.

We had another clean exchange as our lead extended down the back straight and into the final turn. Now, my palms were sweating like crazy because the only way we could lose the race was if I blew the lead—usually, each team's fastest runners ran the anchor legs. As my teammate hit his mark, I took off. After six or seven steps, I threw my right hand back and yelled, "Stick!" I received the baton cleanly, and started rounding the curve toward the finish line.

As I rounded the final turn, out of the hundreds of people who were there, I heard one voice above all others. It was my dad, yelling, "Go, Spencer! Go, Spencer! Go, Spencer!" We won the race, but what I will always remember more than the victory is the sacrifice that my dad made for me that day.

If you are a father, give your kids every chance to become successful by instilling in them the values and ethics they'll need to make a tangible contribution to society. Accept responsibility as the role model in your family; don't leave the task to school-teachers, recording artists and professional athletes.

Step Three: Application

Successfully understanding and applying the three biblical principles we looked at above—the law of labor, the law of reaping and sowing, and the law of instruction—will help you further develop your leadership abilities. However, steps one and two of leadership development are useless without step three. If you don't apply what you've learned, what good will that information be?

Some people are still in the starting blocks of life, meaning that they are still waiting for the race to begin. They're stretching, adjusting their wristbands, checking the direction of the wind and refilling their water bottles. In short, they are stuck in steps one and two. Now, it's time for you to get out of the starting blocks and start running! And doing that is simple, really. Leaders make things happen, and that is all you have to do. Find two or three important things that you want to accomplish in your life right now, and begin developing the action steps you'll need to take to make them happen.

As you begin to apply yourself—and as you read this book—try to be as transparent as possible. Really make an honest assessment of your present life and where you want to be in the future. Then, each day, make small, incremental steps toward the goals that you have set.

But be realistic about your goals. Know what you are capable of accomplishing, and don't set yourself up for automatic failure. Some people set such unrealistic goals when starting a new venture that it would be virtually impossible for anyone to reach them. Then, when the reality sets in and they see that they're going to fall a little short in reaching those goals, they blame the opportunity, their team, their dog or any other excuse that's handy at the moment.

In a situation like this, of course, there's nothing wrong with the people or their teams; more than likely, they just happened to set goals that were a little too far out of their reach. Don't do this yourself. Don't say that you want to be debt-free, or have the biggest team in company history. Instead, concentrate on the smaller goals you must first achieve in order to reach those overall targets. The more specific you can be about your goal, the greater the chance you have of making significant progress toward achieving it.

For example, in our seminars, we often ask who in the audience would like to achieve financial freedom, and many people raise their hands. Everybody wants to become wealthy and can envision themselves leading the lifestyle of a wealthy person.

However, you can't just raise your hand and say, "Yes, I want to be rich!" and then go back to work at your job for the next twenty years. Insanity has been defined as doing the same thing over and over again and expecting a different result; *you* must do something different. Becoming financially independent is a great goal, but how will you go about achieving it?

I'll tell you: First, you must a find a vehicle that will release your potential to earn more money. And to find that, you must be open to new opportunities. The irony behind the success of The 3 CEOs is that none of us thought that our financial independence would come from network marketing. Honestly, I thought it was an industry for people who couldn't get real jobs, and why would I waste the hundreds of thousands of dollars that had gone into my education to promote an opportunity with a multi-level business model?

But I was ignorant of the potential that existed in this industry. The more research I did, the more I discovered that network marketing creates more millionaires than any other industry in the world! You don't have to have a degree to figure out that with the convergence of the right opportunity and the right time, lots of money can be made.

I have a word of advice to my fellow "ignorant" professionals who believe that network marketing is not for them: Set your advanced degrees and your pride aside, and take a really close look at this industry. Once I did, I saw a legitimate, powerful form of business that could be my vehicle toward financial freedom. Years later, with a lot of experience and success under my belt, I feel as if I've broken out of the matrix, and it's become my duty to free as many other people as I can!

Recruiting Leaders

To build a massive organization in the industry of network marketing, you must be adept at recruiting. Most people will never tell you this, but there is an art and even a science to it. Since becoming involved in networking, I've read numerous books that suggest talking to everyone you see in order to recruit as many people as possible, but I disagree with this philosophy. Recruiting, I believe, has to be strategic.

It's been said that network marketing is for anyone, and that's true—but it's not for *everyone*, and you should not be trying to enlist every person you see. This industry is based primarily upon personal relationships. In fact, another name for network marketing is *relationship* marketing. This means that you should get to know something about the people you're recruiting, such as their strengths and weaknesses, their goals in life and, of course, their goals in business. When you begin your new opportunity, don't just recruit anyone you pass on the street. Don't go and get a bunch of business cards and flyers, station yourself at the local mall and harass the shoppers about your new money-making deal, hoping that some of them will bite. I guarantee you will not build a lasting organization this way.

Don't believe me? Then how about a true 3 CEOs story to back it up? On one of our tours, we successfully signed up several professional football players (to preserve confidentiality, we won't divulge their names or the name of their team, but I will say that it was situated in California, south of Los Angeles and slightly north of Mexico). Despite our admonishing them to the contrary, these highly paid superstars spent about $3,000 on making flyers and rented a hotel room to accommodate 200 people. Then, they swarmed the parking lots of local malls and placed their flyers on all the windshields, inviting hundreds of people they'd never met to an upcoming 3 CEOs opportunity meeting.

Now, who wouldn't jump at the chance to meet pro football players and go into business with the local team? Theirs was a great idea, right? Wrong! A whopping four people showed up at the hotel on the night of the presentation, and our players learned a valuable lesson: Introduce your opportunity to people you know first. When you're talking to someone with whom you already have a relationship, they're more likely to trust you and listen to what you have to say—and based on that, they're more likely to give the opportunity a chance. You'll have a much higher success rate recruiting people you are comfortable around than strangers you've never even met.

However, this doesn't mean that you should try to recruit everyone you know. Again, network marketing is for anyone, but you have to be able to recognize when someone—even a person you like and trust—is just not right for the opportunity. To build a lasting empire in this industry, first look for people who are inherently interested in your product. In other words, if you are involved in a travel-related opportunity, present it to people who you know like to travel. Get the idea?

Also, look for people who have a large circle of influence and a great work ethic. Often, you'll find these qualities in business owners and entrepreneurs. Why? Because individuals in this group, more than most, understand the difficulties involved in starting a business and will be more consistent in their approach.

Finally—and this is probably most important—you want to look for people who you know have the money to get started in business *right now*. Remember, you're not starting a business to make friends or to bulk up your résumé. Businesspeople go into business to make money, and that is what you must do. Treat your opportunity like the financial vehicle it is, and be realistic about using it as such.

Now, here's a shocker for you: Sometimes, you can actually be *too* close to the people to whom you want to introduce your opportunity. For example, let's say that you've been working as a nurse for over five years when, all of sudden, you hear about a great company with a product that complements your lifestyle. You agree to join as a representative and are eager to get started, and want everyone you know to be just as excited as you are.

That's great. That's a good attitude to have. But remember that when you start out on this venture, you're asking your friends and family to make a major adjustment in how they perceive you professionally. Most of them already recognize you as a medical professional, not as a representative in a networking venture, and the change could be difficult for some to make.

This is especially true of family members. In fact, we suggest that your relatives, for the most part, should be the last people that you ask to get involved in your new opportunity. Why? Because you can be too close to your brothers and sisters, aunts, uncles, cousins and so on. This group is not your "warm" market—they are actually your "hot" market. They want and need to see the physical manifestations of your success (i.e., the cars, the houses, the clothes and the jewelry that they associate with financial freedom) before they will even think about joining your team. They may take months or even years to join, if they ever do.

But don't be offended if and when this happens. Though you might be a little disappointed when your kin don't seem as excited about network marketing as you are, as a leader, you have to just move on to the next prospect—and give your family members a call every $10,000 or so, just to see if they're interested yet!

Recruiting Up

Recruiting up is the practice of talking to people who are simply perceived as winners—people who are successful by traditional standards. These people may have a better job than you; they may drive a nicer car and make more money. They may seem intimidating, but if you want to build a massive organization, you can only do so by talking to the most dynamic people you know. These are the people you definitely want on your team.

Every major player in networking will tell you that recruiting up is the secret sauce in the networking recipe. As The 3 CEOs, we make it a daily practice, and so should you. We're like professional scouts in pro sports, constantly evaluating talent and looking for people with a high "it" factor—an intangible quality, that special something that you just can't seem to figure out. It's the extra spring in a person's step, the gleam in her eye, the air of confidence that always seems to surround her. It's a certain swagger.

People with a high "it" factor seem to light up any room into which they walk. They command attention, and people listen to what they have to say. They have an unspoken confidence that tells the rest of the world, "Look out, here I come!"

For example, Floyd has an extremely high "it" factor. I remember one day when Donald and I were conducting a training, and Floyd happened to walk into the room. The hundreds of guests in attendance broke into applause before Floyd even uttered a word. His "it" factor caused quite a reaction!

Many people's network marketing organizations suffer because they are intimidated by the idea of recruiting up. But remember, successful people got that way by looking at and being open to new opportunities, and some people are poor for a reason. One great acronym for the word "poor" is "passing over opportunities repeatedly," and that is exactly what you must *not* do. The very person who you think will join your opportunity won't, and the one who you think won't join will, so never be afraid to approach someone and ask—no matter how successful or wealthy they may be.

Of course, we don't mean to say that recruiting up is easy. There *is* a skill to it. To attract a recruit with a high "it" factor, there must be something attractive about you. I don't mean that you have to be handsome or pretty—I mean *professionally* attractive. Successful people evaluate you and your credibility within seconds, based on criteria such as:

- How you are dressed
- How well-groomed you are
- If you appear desperate for new business partners
- Your nervous and insecure behavior.

Before you even utter a word, these people may have already made a decision as to whether or not they are going to listen to anything you have to say. This happened to Floyd, Donald and me after having breakfast at a restaurant one morning. As we prepared to get into our car, a gentleman came over and asked if three sharp guys such as ourselves would be interested in making some additional money. We played along, though we were all thinking the same thing: This guy looked a few biscuits away from being homeless! His clothes were disheveled, and the sole of his right shoe was having a conversation with the left one. To make matters worse, he suggested that we wait while he went to his car to get a magazine and a brochure about his "life-changing" opportunity. Unfortunately, it seemed as though along the way, he'd forgotten to change his own life.

The point is, this man's opportunity may have in fact been wonderful, but his initial impression was so unattractive that if we ever did decide to join the opportunity, it most certainly would not have been with him!

How Do I Know When I Have a Good Prospect?

Here is a formula that you can use to determine whether or not you have a good prospect or recruit:

$$Opportunity + \text{``Why''} = Good\ Prospect$$

Let me explain. When a person joins the opportunity with a significant "why"—a significant reason for joining in the first place—then you have a good recruit. Everyone's "why" is different; yours might be quitting that second job or being able to bring your spouse home full-time. Someone else's might be putting their kids in private school or earning money for a down-payment on a new home. Whatever your "why" is, it must be personal and more significant than just money. And, above all else, it must be large. It must be something that you want in your life pretty badly.

The plus sign in the above equation indicates that for a person to be a good prospect, both elements—your opportunity and your prospect's "why"—must exist at the same time. If they don't, then this person is just another body in your business, another person who joins up and then does nothing with it for quite some time. It takes something happening in his or her life to make that "why" larger—such as job loss, illness or financial hardship—to transform him or her into a good recruit.

And a *good* recruit can become a *great* recruit. Here is the formula for that:

$$Opportunity + \text{“Why”} + Time = Great\ Prospect$$

Notice that I have now added a third element to the equation: time. A great recruit joins the opportunity, has a strong "why" and has the time to work the business. With all three factors in place, you have a potentially great prospect! Why? Because when most people join an opportunity, they are still working a traditional job that requires a majority of their time and attention. If you look at the real superstar networkers, however, they each had ample time to dedicate to growing their networking businesses.

And don't forget: Once you identify a great recruit on your team, you want to train, nurture and cultivate that individual because he or she could be a budding superstar in your organization!

Leadership by Being "Coachable"

The "team" concept that we've used to build an organization consisting of tens of thousands of people is similar to the approach used in sports. In basketball, for example, an organization may have one outstanding player—a "superstar," such as Michael Jordan—but that one player will never beat an entire, organized unit of team members working together. No matter how great the superstar is, no matter what kind of skills he has, he will still have to work with the other players if he wants to win the game.

This sort of teamwork starts with the idea of each player being coachable. Every superstar in professional sports, from

Emmitt Smith to Wayne Gretzky to Jackie Joyner-Kersee, has had to work under the direction of a coach. Even the world's greatest golfer, Tiger Woods, has a coach to give him advice and help him work on his weak areas.

In the industry of network marketing, it's much the same. Talent alone won't allow you to reach your full potential as a leader; it must be harnessed and cultivated by someone who knows what to do with it. To be a great leader, you first need to follow, and you must start by finding a great coach or a mentor to assist you.

But what should you look for in a coach? That's a great question. It's easy to get trapped by people who think that they are coaches, though, in reality, they are more like micromanaging tyrants. They lord over your organization and make unrealistic demands on both you and your team. They treat you more like an unappreciated employee than a partner in the business.

Good coaches, on the other hand, have credibility and have attained a documented level of success. An example is Phil Jackson, who won several world championships coaching Michael Jordan with the Chicago Bulls. After Michael retired, Phil still had a desire to coach and looked to the Los Angeles Lakers, who at the time had a young, rising superstar named Kobe Bryant on the team. Kobe had lots of potential, and could probably achieve greatness if he had the right coach—and he did so with Phil Jackson, who won the respect of the egotistical prodigy simply because he had the achievements to back up what he said.

Next, a good coach will tell you what you need to hear, though it may not necessarily be what you *want* to hear. Many people would rather be spoiled by praise than saved by criticism and if you're one of them, this coaching method might challenge you from time to time.

As Floyd, Donald and I coach our teams, we push people just

far enough to test their will and determination, but not so far as to crush their enthusiasm. This requires some understanding and appreciation of the individual talents of the people in our organization. Different people respond to different challenges differently; some people you can really push and be direct with, while others need a more philosophical approach. Either way, with proper instruction, the outcome can be the same.

One of the most important things to remember is that the coach-player relationship is a two-way street. There are some qualities that the coach must have, but there are also some things that the player—in this case, your recruit—must do to reach the desired goal. First, the recruit must possess some level of humility. You can't coach a "know it all" or someone who already has all the answers. Think about this: Tiger Woods, despite having already won eight majors (including the unprecedented four in a row in 2000–2001) and thirty-nine tour titles, believed he could get better—so much so that he hired a new coach and developed a completely different swing. Amidst Tiger's talent, dominance and confidence was an inner humility that led him to seek the advice and counsel of a third party.

Likewise, Michael Jordan had to have the inner humility to listen to Phil Jackson's instructions. Sure, Michael always knew that he could out-jump, out-score and out-rebound Phil at any time, but that's not the point. Michael wasn't trying to dominate Phil Jackson; he was trying to dominate the other twenty-nine teams that were trying to beat him during the course of the NBA season. He understood that there were things that Phil could see from a coach's perspective that he could not because he was too close to the action.

In sports, as in business and in life, a winner is never comfortable or satisfied. As talented as you might think you are, you can always get better; sometimes, you just have to be able to get yourself out of the way. Many people's frustrations about why their businesses are not growing can be resolved simply by looking in the mirror, though I know that's a difficult thing to do. It takes a lot of humility to accept that you have flaws that need to be worked out, but we all have them, and it's something that we all have to do.

I remember meeting one dynamic couple who was building a wonderful organization. Their team was growing, and they were reaching some great milestones in the company. Then, all of a sudden, the momentum just stopped. On one of our tours, we were able to witness the couple in action at one of their weekly meetings, and we instantly saw the problem: The husband was talking way too long and in fact was turning the presentation into more of a church service than a business meeting.

Despite our recommendations that his wife, who was a much better presenter with a calmer and more attractive demeanor, conduct the presentations and that he assume a more supportive role, they persisted in doing it their own way. Their organization, as you can guess, continued to suffer lethargic growth because of the husband's unwillingness to run the play that the coach had called and get himself out of the way. Remember, being coachable in business is a major key to ultimately becoming a great leader.

Donald's View

Following the Leader

The first rule of being a good leader is that you must be a good follower. In both life and business, you must learn how to crawl before you can walk and finding someone you can look up to and emulate should be the first step you take toward becoming a great leader yourself.

Two of the most important qualities you should look for in a leader when you are trying to become one yourself are credibility and documentation—meaning that he or she should already have accomplished some of the things that you desire, and have something to show for it. Don't ever let anyone tell you what to do unless they have tangible evidence of their own hard work and achievement.

When you do find someone who's qualified, it's imperative to get yourself out of the way and follow that person's instructions. Put your ego aside and really *listen* to what your leader—also known as your mentor—has to tell you. This person has already "been there, done that," and undoubtedly learned a lot along the way. The best things you can do are open your ears, take a lot of notes, and heed whatever advice they want to give you.

Now, keep in mind that network marketing is about replication, not innovation. The idea is to take your mentor's ideas and use them for yourself—not to use them as a basis for your own new and different plan for financial freedom. If someone who has made a million dollars is willing to tell you exactly how they did it, you'd be wise to follow that advice to the letter if you want the same results. Anything else would be like buying a McDonald's franchise and painting your arches green.

The goal of a good leader is to develop others into future leaders—that's what your mentor is interested in doing. It makes sense, doesn't it? The more good leaders an already good leader has, the more successful his or her business will be—and the more good leaders that second generation can go on to train, and so on and so on. It's an exponential business, you could say, and one that really rewards you depending on what you put into it.

The most common mistake I see people making in network marketing is violating this concept of following the leader. Even people who are brand new to the industry often believe that they can figure it out on their own and take charge of a business that they do not yet understand. It's not surprising, really—many of those who come into network marketing are leaders in other areas of their lives, so it's only natural that they automatically want to take charge of their new businesses, too. They're supervisors at work, or little league coaches, or members of a board of trustees, and they think that they already know how to run things successfully. But that's the thing—they just *think* they do. In this business, you must develop your leadership skills before anything else, and you can only do that by learning the business from someone who knows it well.

Personal Development

After you find a good coach or mentor, your journey toward becoming a great leader yourself can get underway. The first and most important step in this process is concentrating on personal development. This involves looking deep inside yourself to find your real skills, talents *and* weaknesses, and then working to strengthen them so that when you do become a leader, you'll come into it full-strength. Of course, we all have room for improvement, but if you want to be a successful leader with a thriving business, you have to be as close to the top of your game as you can.

Of course, if your mentor tells you that you should be in possession of a particular quality that you do not already have, you should find a way to go out there and develop it. Do you lack self-confidence? Read some self-help books or attend a motivational seminar. Are you a bit of a procrastinator? Google the phrase "time management" and you'll find almost 17,000 Websites to offer you advice in that area. Whatever it is you need to work on, be proactive about it. Don't just sit there and wait for the information to come to you because, chances are, it won't.

Some fundamentals that I would advise you to explore while working on your personal development are:

- **Empathy.** Remember that network marketing is a business of relationships, and it's important for you to do what's best for your associates, even if it's not what's best for you. If one of them has rent due on Friday, don't ask her to put $500 into the business on Wednesday with a promise that she'll have double that in a week. Her rent isn't due in a week; it's due on *Friday*. In a case like that, it might be better for you to tell her that she should forget about network marketing for a minute and focus on a job with a steady paycheck.

People don't care what you know until they know that you care. If your reps know that you have their best interests at heart, they will follow you even when they don't fully agree with what you're prescribing. A good leader can stretch his followers because he has worked to gain their trust.

- **Insight**. As a leader, it pays for you to find the advantages that each of your associates possesses. Not everyone's skills are immediately apparent; sometimes, you have to get to know a person pretty well before you can tell where their hidden talents lie. A great leader knows how to bring out the best in people, and when you can do this with your associates, you're on your way toward building a successful team.

  The same goes for when you're recruiting. Instead of just inviting everyone you meet to join the business, you should get some idea of what they can bring to it first. Everyone has some sort of competitive advantage within them; it's up to you to find out what it is, and determine if you can use it.

- **Drive.** This almost goes without saying. To be the best, the saying goes, you have to beat the best; to be a great leader, you have to know more than the next person knows, and know it earlier, faster and better. Obtaining new information is imperative and you've always got to have your eyes and ears open. You should be going to seminars, talking to mentors and other successful people in the industry, and doing whatever you can to maintain a connection with what's going on in your team, your business, and the industry at large.

Being a good leader means having the strength to tell people what to do and how to do it, but it also means having the wisdom to recognize those who can lead themselves. If you were a coach, how would you lead Michael Jordan? Probably just by giving him a ball first and seeing what he's got. If Michelangelo came to paint your house, you certainly wouldn't tell him how to hold his brush, would you? A leader recognizes when a person has expertise in an area and leaves it alone; though it may seem counterintuitive, backing off when you need to is an important method of building the strongest team you can.

That may seem like a paradox, and it is—and it's not the only one when it comes to leadership. Another is that leaders have to be both hungry and humble; they have to want it all but be modest when they get it, concentrating more on whatever comes next than on flaunting their newfound success. Another leadership paradox entails learning how to be the voice of authority while still sometimes yielding and making compromises.

But leaders must also work hard to remain true to themselves. Though I admire Floyd and Spencer, and value all the advice they give me, I do not try to be exactly like them. I can't be; I don't have the same experiences, knowledge or skills that make them uniquely *them*. Just like a guard on a basketball team shouldn't be out in the middle, banging up with Shaquille and trying to get rebounds, we all must know our places. And instead of trying to be someone we can't, especially as leaders, we must concentrate on being the best versions of ourselves that we can be. People spend too much time wanting to be someone else, and that's not what personal development is about.

The number-one most important thing that any leader can do is lead by example. I would never recommend that one of my associates do something I can't or won't do myself, and you should never ask others to do things that you have not done. If you do, you will quickly lose credibility with them and a team that does not believe in you is not going to make your business grow.

Part of leading by example is knowing your business better than the people who follow you. As I mentioned earlier, you have to know more than the next guy; you must keep current on new developments and continue to grow as a leader. Don't be afraid of change, and take responsibility for challenging situations. You must always conquer any fears that you may have.

For example, public speaking is said to be the most common fear that people have—more common even than the fear of death. This is a huge drawback in the network marketing industry where, to be a great leader, you have to be comfortable in front of large audiences. For a person who is just starting out, that could consist of just five people, but once you practice on a group of that size, it gets a little easier, and you can move on to ten people. And as you build your confidence, you can challenge yourself to do even more.

I even had a problem with this myself. When I first started out in network marketing, I cringed at the thought of speaking in front of so many people. I was so scared that I would think of any excuse to get out of giving a presentation—that is, until Floyd, my mentor, told me that the one who speaks in front of the room makes the most money. I realized that what he said was true, and I knew that I had to conquer my biggest fear.

So, I studied and practiced, and then studied and practiced some more. My leaders, Floyd and Spencer, gave me a ten-minute piece of their regular sixty-minute presentation, and after each performance, they critiqued what I had done. I followed this routine for six months and, in time, it helped me gain some self-confidence. I became almost comfortable with being in front of a crowd.

And then, one day, they decided to put me out there for the full sixty minutes on my own. We had a presentation scheduled in Columbia, South Carolina, and at the last minute, they found out that they would not able to attend. I thought I was going to die. I was angry and afraid; I felt as though my leaders had failed me. I was never going to forgive them for leaving me alone like that.

But little did I know that chance occurrence would really force me to step up to the plate and take my turn at bat. Taking the stage for that hour-long presentation, I realized that it was my time to become the leader I was meant to be. Fortunately, I had seen my leaders present dozens of times, and I tried to emulate what I'd seen them do, keeping in mind that the team was counting on me to bring home the gold.

And I did great! My confidence level was at an all time high— especially when I later learned that someone new had joined the business after hearing my presentation. With that under my belt, I couldn't wait to try it again. A leader had been born, and I finally had developed the confidence I needed to present on my own. I truly believe that this experience was the foundation that allowed me to develop in so many other ways.

From that day forward, I scheduled event after event, no longer relying on Floyd and Spencer's help. The thing I had feared the most had become my strongest tool and to this day, I work to sharpen that tool every chance I get. Once *you* begin to conquer your fears, you'll be on your way as well. When you gain control over the things that hold you back, nothing else can stop you. The best advice I can give you is to go down your list of fears, work on overcoming them, and check them off one at a time. Boldly chip away at the list until your fears become your strengths.

Recruiting Your Future Leaders

Recruiting is part of being a leader, and every leader has his or her own style. Currently, I'm looking for people with real business strength. I want people who have experience in corporate America, which is one of the best training grounds there is. While working for other people's companies, individuals learn valuable skills that they can transfer to their own businesses. By the time they get the opportunity to become entrepreneurs, they often find that they already know how to do the work that it requires.

However, for all their skills in administration, meeting deadlines, doing reports and teambuilding, many are not comfortable with doing it all for themselves. They're so used to giving their talents away in return for a weekly paycheck that the possibility of entrepreneurship seems like a dream—and a daunting one at that. They have to get past the security of what they have before they can move ahead and make something of themselves.

Another problem is that so many people desire to have more in life but haven't yet found the vehicle that will propel them in that direction. They're hungry to learn, to get out of the rat race and better themselves, and are willing to do what it would take to get them there. As a leader, this could be where you would come in, with information about the opportunity they need.

But not all of my associates come from corporate America. There are individuals in all walks of life who are perfectly suited to the network marketing arena but just don't know it yet. Once, I met a man at an airport who built barns for a living. He'd struck up a conversation with me, to be honest, because he'd noticed my suit and thought that I must do something important. We talked for a while and I could tell, from the passion and excitement with which he spoke of his job, that he would have been a great candidate for network marketing.

Instead of restricting your recruitment efforts to a certain sector or area, keep your mind open when it comes to finding potential reps. Focus instead on some core qualities—good personality, strong work ethic, an interest in self-development, a desire for financial freedom. Individuals in possession of these certainly have at least some potential worth investigating.

When I talk to people about my network marketing opportunity, I don't feel like it's *recruiting*. Honestly, I feel more like I'm saving people's lives. I'm offering them the lifestyle that they were made for, that they desire, and all they have to do is admit that they want to be financially free. I don't plaster telephone poles with flyers or leave postcards underneath windshield wipers; I simply talk to people. I have conversations. I'm not *recruiting* them; I'm throwing them a lifeline and giving them the opportunity that they've been looking for, even if they didn't know it before.

You could say that I "recruit" just by going out day to day, through the natural operations of my life. As I go about my business, however, I keep my eyes open—I'm always looking for people who are looking for me. I don't believe in coincidence; I believe that people meet each other for a reason, a season or a lifetime, and that it's up to them to figure out which it is—and what the reason is, if that's the case.

An example that comes to mind involves an old friend who called me one day just to see how I was doing, though we hadn't seen or spoken to each other in years. Was that simple chance? Or was God trying to tell me something? Personally, I believe the latter, that God knew that this person needed something from me, and that I needed something from him. When I told him that I'd stumbled upon an opportunity that had made me financially independent, and he said that he was at a point in his life where he was looking for the same—well, then I knew what the reason was.

Things like this happen to me all the time. Often, I run into people, it seems, on purpose. Years ago, I was at an airport and was talking with a young lady who worked in corporate America. She confided in me that she wanted to have her own ministry and be a public speaker. Well...did I have an opportunity for her! She eagerly joined my business—and so did her husband—and now has a team of her own that is several hundred members strong.

When I meet people this way, I never start a conversation with, "I'm in network marketing. Would you like to join my team?" Instead, I just go with the natural course of conversation and listen to the other person's needs. As a leader, you must always ask a potential representative, "How can *I* help *you*?" Just as I want to know what skills a person could offer my organization, I want understand what he or she needs in his life, and how I might be able to provide it. In this business, I get paid to help others, and the better they do, the better I do. The more I help people get what they want, the more I get what I want. So, I focus on their needs.

People are always talking about where they're going and where they went—and after about fifteen minutes, they *always* start to talk about money. I get to know a lot about people just by listening to them, and as always, I try to assess what their needs are, and how I might be able to help them. Just as often as not, they may not need my business, and that's fine. I don't bother people like that with my card or with overtures to bring them in. I'm looking for people to help, but the truth is, not everyone needs it. Not everyone needs *business*. Some people just need to get a job.

Besides, it's just plain unattractive when people try to shove something down your throat, especially when it's something that you're not looking for. If I'm talking to someone and see a need for us to have a second conversation about business, I'll try to set it up—if that goes with the natural flow. I've never invited anyone into my business for whom I didn't think it would work.

I realize that my style is a little different than what people expect from network marketers. It's true, there are people in the industry who just want to go out and get fifteen names in a day, regardless of their potential. Personally, I rely strictly on meeting people for a reason because I believe it increases my credibility, which can sometimes be the key to success. Think about it: If you and I had a very respectful relationship, and you saw me as a credible person, and I got involved in something that did well for me, you'd want to investigate it for yourself, wouldn't you? On the other hand, if I'm trying to give you a business card while I'm a guest at your wedding or seated next to you on an airplane—a captive audience if there ever was one—I doubt that you would have much respect for me at all. You never get a second chance once you put a bad taste in someone's mouth.

Building a Team of Leaders

The backbone of network marketing is building a big team—no, make that building a strong team. High numbers are great, but they don't mean a thing without quality. Your focus should be not on recruiting as many people as you can but recruiting the best people you can.

To this end, people have to come to your business willingly.

Don't try to trick anyone into joining; don't exaggerate facts and set their expectations too high, or a year from now, they'll all be quitting on you. When I invite people to join, I let them know this is a real business and that if they don't work, they won't get wealthy. I help my people manage their expectations from the beginning because time is more important than money. I don't want to invest in someone and then find out six months to a year later that they can't deliver at the level I need them to. Basically, I tell people the truth.

And because of it, I have a great team made up of thousands of intelligent, motivated, skilled, self-sufficient individuals. But then, I'd expect nothing less, because I helped to mold these leaders in my own image. Network marketing is a replication business; when training a team, you try to reproduce who you are, not who you want to be. I wanted a team that would attack their business and take ownership of it, just as I do with mine. I wanted people who would take responsibility for things that go wrong and fix them if they can—and I got these people, because I was selective about the individuals to whom I offered the opportunity.

My Journey in Personal Development

I have this theory that we all just want to separate ourselves as much as we can from poverty. We each have our own reasons, but in the end, all we want is to be financially free. For me, the reason is my children; the further I can get them away from hardship now, the less they will have to worry about it in the future.

Early in my life, I decided that I would do whatever it took to be successful. Growing up in middle-class Baltimore, Maryland, I watched the people around me and decided that my goal in life was not to be a mechanic or some other blue-collar worker. I didn't know how I would get around it, but I knew that I had to and that someday, I would make it happen.

But I also knew that I would have to work for that success.

Early in life, my mom and dad taught me the value of hard work, and told me that no matter what I wanted in life, I would have to work for it. To "earn" my free time, I had to do chores and homework; if I had nothing at all to do, my dad would advise me on something "constructive" that I could do. Sometimes, this involved more chores, but often, he simply told me to read a book; he was very big on reading, and we practically had our own library right in our house. If I didn't feel like reading, that was fine, but I had to find *something* to do. There was no sitting around in my household, and there was a clear distinction made between activity and productivity.

For example: When it snowed, the kids in my neighborhood would grab their sleighs and head for the nearest hill, or have snowball fights out in the street. Not me, though; I had to grab a shovel and clear the sidewalk in front of my home. After I was done with that, I was free to have a blast but there was no question in my mind that work had to come before play. That was what my parents had taught me, and how I developed the incredible work ethic that has gotten me to the point where I am today.

As with anything that is done consistently and repetitively, in time, I got good at shoveling snow and realized that I could turn it into a business. I found that my neighbors would pay me for clearing their walkways after a storm, and for the first time, I experienced working and getting paid for it. Immediately, I fell in love.

As I grew, I looked for other opportunities to make my own money. I would go to the grocery store and help people get their bags to their cars; sometimes, they'd tip me a quarter, or sometimes, even a dollar or two. Regardless of how much they gave me, I was happy. I was working; I was being productive instead of active. The money, though I liked it, was just a bonus to the self-esteem it gave me.

At the age of twelve, I became a paper delivery boy. I did it by myself for a while, and as with everything else, I took pride in what I did. I made sure that the papers were delivered on time and that I was courteous when collecting the customers' payments. I built a good relationship with each and every one of them, and I felt a good deal of pride in the little business I'd built.

And in time, because I'd done so well, I was given more and more responsibility. My route grew so big that at one point, I had to hire my best friend to help me out—my first foray, it seemed, into networking. I really enjoyed this job and my first experience with being a manager of sorts but after a few years, I felt as though I was outgrowing it and started to look for something else. As usual, I always sought to go to the next level, and I never, ever quit unless it was to go on to a better opportunity.

At sixteen, I was old enough to work at McDonald's and I got a job there, cooking hamburgers. While most of the other kids I worked with hated their jobs, I made the best of mine because, as my dad always said, "If you have to be a street sweeper, be the best street sweeper you can." So, I flipped those burgers with a smile, and did my best to make my customers happy.

To keep things from getting boring in this repetitive, sort of mind-numbing job, I tried to set up challenges for myself whenever I could. Though most people hated it, I loved to see buses pull into the parking lot because I knew it meant a lot of customers at once. I would see how fast I could serve them all, trying to beat my "record" every time.

When I felt as though I had to make a step up from McDonald's, I moved on to a job at a department store. Instead of a uniform, I wore a shirt and tie and instead of cooking fast food, I assisted customers in the shoe department. Of course, I became the best shoe salesman I could possibly be, going above and beyond what the job actually called for when it came to serving my customers. I did so well that before long, I was able to secure a position with the company's customer service department. I stayed there all through high school, only quitting when I had something else to move on to.

And that something else was the Air Force. This, as you can imagine, was a challenge like none I had ever experienced before. I was eighteen years old and leaving home for the first time, going thousands of miles away just for boot camp. My first night there, in San Antonio, Texas, I laid on my bunk, thinking about how maybe I should have gone to college. For the first time, I wasn't completely self-confident. I even actually cried myself to sleep.

But the next morning, after the shock of being away from home had worn off, I woke up with a different perspective. I didn't love the situation any more, but I reminded myself that I was not a quitter. I had made a four-year commitment to the military, and I had to honor that, so I resolved to make the best of it. The challenge, I decided, was on.

Everything about the Air Force made me grow up, and fast. I developed personally in so many ways, in body, mind and soul. Boot camp in particular stretched me in a way I would never have imagined because as stern as my parents were, I had always felt their love; here, no one was nurturing me. In boot camp, you either did what you were told, or you didn't and, pretty much, the choice was always the former. I was up every morning at 4:45 and gone until nine at night. It was a time of nonstop activity.

Boot camp was like a vigorous, all-day workout for body and soul. Discipline was the key—I had to have self-control like you wouldn't believe, or I never would have made it. I couldn't complain about the hard work, or I'd be given more; I couldn't negotiate an exercise because I thought there was a better way to do it. I had to hold my tongue instead of speaking out, as I was used to doing. It was difficult to get used to, but a great lesson I learned about self-control.

Boot camp was a place that I literally had to survive, and

survive I did. When I was through there, I moved on to tech school in Rantoul, Illinois, at Chanute Air Force Base, where I learned to work on electrical systems on aircraft. I really enjoyed tech school because I loved learning; I'd chalk that up to all those books my dad had made me read as a kid when I had nothing else better to do with my time.

The next stop in my military career was my permanent assignment at Myrtle Beach Air Force Base, where I worked on airplanes. I was also able to make new friends and have a little fun once in a while, which was a great relief after the lack of fun I'd experienced at boot camp. After getting familiar with my duties at the base and getting into a nice routine, I was even able to think about what else I wanted to do with my life. I'd realized, since joining the Air Force, that the military would not be my life. But what else could I possibly want to do?

I decided that to begin with, I had to get a college degree and as soon as I could, I enrolled in some classes at Coastal Carolina, an on-base branch of the University of South Carolina. I would work on planes all day, then go to class at night; it was a hell of a schedule, but it certainly kept me busy—and productive, not just active, as my dad had taught me. Sometimes, it was hard getting through a workday and trying to focus on my studies at the same time, but at that point in my life, my goals and desires were coming into clearer focus, and I knew that I had to push ahead as much as I could. I had to take as many classes as I could while I was still on active duty, so I could get out of the Air Force and go on to college full-time.

The good news was that once that happened, I would have the GI Bill to pay my college expenses, though I would need to have money on which to live. So, while in the Air Force, I concentrated on saving money to live on later, while I was in school, by going back to my roots, so to speak—I got a job at McDonald's again. My plan was to make some extra money there that I could live off of while saving my military pay to use later on.

So, every morning, I got up extra early and went off the base to work the opening shift at the local McDonald's. With just the income I made there, I was able to pay off my car in a short period of time, continue with my college courses and save my Air Force paycheck. It was hard work, and a lot of work, but again, as my parents had taught me, it was the only way to go to achieve my dreams.

Finally, the day arrived when my contract with the Air Force was fulfilled, and I was released. Sticking to my plan, I moved to the main campus of the University of South Carolina in Columbia, where I set right to pursuing a four-year degree. Unable, I guess, to completely let go of my military training, I also enlisted in the South Carolina Air National Guard.

College was different from anything else I had done in my life up until that point. I had been used to living with my parents and doing whatever they told me to do, and then being in the Air Force, where practically every minute of my day was planned and regimented. In college, no one forced me to do anything. Everything was optional. I could go to class if I wanted to, or not go; I could do my homework if I wanted to, or not do it. If I did these things, I would do well in school; if I didn't, my grades would suffer. This was not a hard concept to grasp. But the point was that for the first time, the choice was *mine*. I could feel absolutely free to fail, if I wanted to.

But thankfully, I didn't, because my work ethic wouldn't allow it. All those Saturday mornings I'd spent as a kid cleaning the house instead of sleeping, and all that self-control I'd practiced and mastered in boot camp finally came to fruition here. Though the temptation to slack off and not do all that was expected of me as a student was great, everything I'd been taught so far told me that it wasn't the right thing to do—and so, I didn't.

My first semester of school was great. I loved my classes, and I couldn't get enough of learning all this new information. Unfortunately, after that short period of time, Operation Desert Storm began and because I was in the National Guard, I was pulled out of school to go to war. I was sent to Saudi Arabia, where I was met with a new kind of challenge—a true test of my ability to survive. Would I live or would I die? I had no way of predicting that either way.

This part of my life was marked by long, hot days and cold, short nights. To keep my mind off the gravity of the situation, I often thought about what I was going to do when I got back home, including finishing my education and maybe starting a business. Though I was at war, and stuck in the middle of a strange land, I tried to view it as nothing more than another growth stage in my personal development.

Fortunately, I made it through my tour of duty, and I was never happier than I was on the day a plane took me back to South Carolina. I arrived at home with a greater respect for life and an even greater drive to succeed. I returned to school, received my degree, and found the love of my life—my wife, Deborah, with whom I was ready to start a family.

We married right out of college and moved to New Jersey, where I'd landed my first real job, with a company called Dudley Products, Inc., a company that provided hair care products to hairstylists. This was another new challenge for me; I was joining a sales force made up of the 162 best salespersons alive. I was a sales manager, responsible for servicing areas in Philadelphia and parts of New Jersey; my job was to develop new markets and maintain existing accounts.

From my first day with the company, I had a strong desire to be the best distributor I could possibly be. And, from the first day, that required a good deal of hard work and dedication on my part. I had my share of difficult days, especially when I was new to the field but, as I had been taught by my parents, I never, ever gave up. I knew that this was the job that was feeding my family, and I took that more seriously than anything.

During my first year at Dudley Products, my first child was born—a son, Brandon Bradley, who immediately became my "why"—my reason for wanting to excel. I wanted this little boy to have a life that I could be proud of, and I knew he was depending totally on me. I understood how great this responsibility was, and instead of shrinking away from it, I stepped up to the plate. I was ready to do whatever I had to do.

Deborah and I went on to have three more children, each about twenty-two months apart.. In the end, we had a perfect package of two boys and two girls: Brandon, Brian, Bryce and Brooke. Having four beautiful children who counted on me every day to make it happen gave me reason and purpose like I had never known in my life. With each birth, I renewed my vow to my family that I would do whatever it took to give them the security and happiness they deserved.

After two years of working for Dudley Products, I decided, with the blessing and cooperation of my wife, to go out on my own—to start my own business. I was growing tired of making money for someone else, and knew that with all my experience, I had a fighting chance of doing it for myself.

So, Deborah and I moved from New Jersey to Atlanta to start our own distribution company. Though I knew that it was smart to stick with a business that I already knew inside and out, it was hard work nonetheless. Over time, through lots and lots of hard work, dedication and motivation, we were fortunate enough to build a company that allowed us to enjoy a pretty good lifestyle, including private school educations for our kids.

In the beginning, though, it wasn't so glamorous. Deborah and I made all the deliveries ourselves, until we had enough reserves to add one new distributor. We kept on at that pace, doing less and less hands-on work ourselves, until we had nine distributors altogether. This was a long process; just as it is in network marketing, this business was not built up overnight.

When you run your own business, it's one thing to just be good at what you do; proving your skill to others is another animal altogether. I already knew that I had the experience and talent to be successful in the distribution industry; I'd proven that back at Dudley Products, Inc. However, now it was my own game—it was all up to me. Not only did I have to find clients, but I had to show them how good, reliable and effective my business would be for them.

Daily challenges threatened to keep Deborah and me from success in this new business, but we persisted nonetheless. We had our down months, and we had our up months; we saw both debt and profit. Eventually, just from being consistent, persistent and good at what we did, we built our little business into one of the strongest companies in the beauty industry. And in time, we expanded into other states and moved to South Carolina to distribute the number-one-selling hair care line in the nation.

Looking back on that whole process, I can really see it as a crash course in basic leadership. Every day, there was a new test of character and patience for me to overcome with only myself on which to rely. Learning to lead *is* a daily process and this will never be more apparent to you than when you are at the head of your own organization. From that viewpoint, you will see things a whole lot differently.

I truly believe that leaders do evolve. You may think you're a good leader today but in a few years, you could be even better, or even great. I'm a better leader today than I was yesterday, and next week, I'll be better, too. As with many other aspects of building a business, becoming a solid leader takes time and personal investment. You'll only be as good as what you put into it.

There came a point when Deborah and I felt as though we were pretty set. Though we continued to strive every day for something better, for more achievement and success, we recognized that we had done pretty well for ourselves. We had a nice home; we had four cars. Our children were wanting for nothing. And then, our business crashed, and everything we'd worked for, we lost.

Through a shift in the company that we represented, which accounted for over eighty percent of our overall revenue, we lost the contract that had helped us build our company in the first place. Our income was gone; our house was foreclosed on and all of our cars were repossessed. We weren't just back to square one; we were *behind* square one, in a hole that we weren't sure how to dig ourselves out of.

But that didn't stop us from trying. Life had already taught us that when you fall off the mountain, you have to get back up and try to climb it again, and that was what we set out to do with our limited resources. On Deborah's suggestion, we moved back to Atlanta and went back to the basics. We still had our company, and we went after a new contract with a new company; we won it, and began to build everything all over again. It would be another long road toward success, but we kept our eyes on the goal and remained certain that, one day, we would get there.

But still, I kept my eye out for better prospects. I loved having my own business but at the same time, I looked for something new, another vehicle I could use to reach my goals. Toward that end, on February 18, 2005, both Deborah and I got involved in network marketing, with a company selling a product that we already used. We already believed in it, which was important, and remains important to me today—I would never recommend a product to a customer that I would not use myself.

People say that adversity builds character, but I say that adversity *reveals* character. By going through everything we did—

building a business, losing it all, then building it up again—I really found out what I was made of. Instead of giving in and giving up, I rallied as much as I could. I drew on everything my mom and dad had taught me about responsibility, and relied on my work ethic to get me through. And I found that if the time ever comes to rebuild again, I will do whatever it takes to get back on top.

SIDE TWO
TAKING ACTION

Floyd's View

Building a Big Team Through Correct Activity

So far, we've been saying that it's not the size of your team that matters, but the caliber of its members. This holds true: It is better to have a smaller, high quality team than a cast of thousands that doesn't know much about what they're doing.

But the goal, of course, is to have both numbers *and* quality. When you first enter network marketing, it may seem daunting to have to build a huge organization, a team of thousands and thousands of people. And on top of that, those people must be intelligent, hard-working and able to do whatever you need them to in order to grow the business.

Sounds like a tall order, doesn't it? The best way to approach it is to break it down into smaller, more manageable steps, starting with assembling a core team. Think of it like this: If you had to put together a board of directors to help you run a *Fortune 500* company, whom would you choose? Would it be your unemployed or under-employed friends? Would it be a relative who's big on ideas but short on talent, motivation and drive?

The answer is probably not. Though you may like or even love these people, emotions such as these should not come into the picture in network marketing. You want people who are going to get the job done, not people with whom you like to hang out and have a good time. Considering how much is at stake, you have to be more selective about whom you choose for your team. If you recruit and retain the wrong people, you could lose millions of dollars, not to mention valuable time and, possibly, your livelihood.

Even though you're not investing millions in your network marketing business, you should act like you are—your mindset should be the same as Bill Gates' or Donald Trump's. As we've all said before, network marketing is a business just like any other and the less seriously you take it, the less serious your returns from it will be. "You reap what you sow" is an adage that really applies here.

But let's get back to talking about your core team. Without one, you'll never build an organization of any significant size. Every major corporation in existence today can attribute its success to a small nucleus of talented personnel who make all the important things happen. This phenomenon falls under what's known as the Pareto Principle, or the 80-20 rule, which shows that twenty percent of the people in a company or organization will be responsible for eighty percent of its overall success. And your organization will be no different.

As you build your team, you must constantly look for that next core leader to strengthen your team and add to that twenty percent. In the first section of this book, Spencer mentioned the "it" factor, and that's what you have to keep an eye out for here—

that intangible quality in a man or woman that can't be defined in just one or two words. People who possess the "it" factor light up every room they enter. Their résumés are packed with achievements, but they've made every one of them look easy. Some call what they have "charisma," but I don't think it can be defined that way.

Individuals with the "it" factor are the people you want on your core team because they are capable of making monumental strides very quickly. They are the first to attack problems when they arise, and to motivate people to work to the best of their abilities. They seem to inherently know what it takes to make things happen, and are enthusiastic about going out there and doing just that.

As you begin building your team, make sure that you invite the most talented, self-motivated people you know because they will be the ones with the "it" factor you need. Look for men and women who have had success in other arenas, who have started businesses before, worked in corporate America for some time or can bring a good deal of management experience to the team. Look for people with a large circle of influence—people who have a wide range of quality contacts to whom they can promote your business opportunity. Basically, what you're trying to do is find people who are more talented than you are; this is called recruiting up and it's the best method of building your core team.

If you do not already know people like this, you may need to work on yourself in order to find them. Perhaps your own circle of influence is not so wide. Maybe you're lacking something in the charisma and self-confidence department. Whatever it is, find it and change it, and then use it to find the people with the "it" factor that you need.

The first thing you can do, to be honest, is change the circle of people with whom you associate. You may not feel exactly thrilled about the idea; I'm sure that you love your family and friends, and that's just as it should be. But understand that that's not what I'm talking about. You don't have to turn your back on everyone you know who doesn't fit the right profile. You just have to work on knowing more people who do. Go to your family reunions, and hang out with your childhood buddies—keep on doing just like you do. But at the same time, take action to build a new circle of business associations and relationships, so that you can get the results that you desire in building your team.

In network marketing, building a team is a little like a math equation: You have to pull together a team of hundreds in order to find about a half a dozen core leaders who will go on to help you build a team of thousands. Core leaders have the ability to create something from nothing, to generate powerful results through self-motivation and determination. They have the gift of imagination; they can see what is possible before it becomes a reality.

Your core leaders' vision and leadership will create opportunities—events and engagements such as weekly meetings, luncheons and conference calls—that will allow other team members to build their businesses successfully and help accelerate the growth of your team. The rest of the team will then duplicate these practices and, eventually, they will bring hundreds and even thousands of people to your business. In time, your organization will take on a life of its own and continue to grow without much input from you.

Build a Big Team with a Method of Operation

Quite often, while building a network marketing business, people find it very difficult to use their time efficiently because it's such an open-ended equation. Network marketing has no specific job descriptions, and no specified amount of hours that the business must be open each day. As a result, most people simply don't have a way to monitor their businesses properly.

The key to keeping things on track is becoming a master of efficiency. Spencer is like that—when it comes to time management, methods of operation and simply getting things done, he's the go-to guy in The 3 CEOs. He constantly works to ensure that all three of us complete our numerous tasks and objectives and meet critical deadlines. This is the type of person you need watching over your business.

You also need to set down your daily and weekly methods of operation. This means that you have to get organized and make plans to work on your business each day, with goals that you must reach at least weekly. Most people in network marketing just wing it from day to day, hoping for the best, but in my opinion, that's failing to plan, and planning to fail. They're setting themselves up to do poorly from the very beginning.

Your daily method of operation should be written down and should include designs for how much time you will spend each day working on your business, and what you will do during that time. As you come up with this outline, make sure that you keep the main thing the main thing—in other words, plan to spend eighty percent of your time on the aspects of your business that make you money. This includes exposing people to the opportunity, helping your team members expose others to the business, teaching team members to expose people to the business, or actually selling your product or service to a customer. Remember this rule as it relates to proper activity: *If it doesn't make money, it doesn't make sense!*

Set your schedule consistently and be sure to include sufficient time for prospecting, follow-up, training and any other activities that will be beneficial to operating your business. The better you organize your day and your week, the more efficient you will be and the more successful your business will be. Write everything down: how many people you will speak to each day about your business, where you will go each day to work your business, at what time and for how long you will work your business on the phone. The more detailed you can be when planning out your daily and weekly methods of operation, the better results you'll have.

Drive Your Business With Systems

One of the biggest reasons most people can't move from self-employment to entrepreneurship and business ownership is that they do not understand systems, or the processes by which certain tasks will be accomplished. Each component of a system serves to make a task easier, consistent and more efficient.

Every organization that operates efficiently is system-dependent. Let's go back and look at "Joe's" print shop, which I mentioned in the first section of this book. Joe's business was always in a state of emergency because he had not properly developed systems to counteract the unpredictable. When a piece of equipment broke, he didn't have a set procedure for how to finish his work without it. Nor did he have a policy in place for when he had ten jobs in queue and a rush order came in at the last minute. He just seemed to make everything up as he went along, and it really showed. His store, at times, was in chaos, and I'm sure his profits reflected that.

No matter how small or how large your business is, you must prepare yourself for what will and what might happen by developing systems for every aspect of it, from marketing, sales and promotions to quality control. Great companies even have systems in place to *create* predictability and consistency in their operations, not just react to any disruptions in them. Systems are designed to make things run smoothly; why would you not want to have that kind of insurance in the business you're running?

The great thing about network marketing is that the systems have already been put in place by the company for which you work and its top leaders. Chances are, the company has been around for a while and has already learned the right way to do things, and that saves you the problem of figuring it out for yourself. All you have to do is follow the systems that already exist, and promote them consistently to your team.

The key here is duplication—you want to do what has already been proven successful, and you want the members of your team to do the same. Creating weekly meetings for your entire team and allowing them to bring guests is a duplicatible system; anyone can plug into it and experience results quickly. The same goes for weekly conference calls, home meetings and team trainings. All of these methods serve as systems that will help you grow and improve your business. When you fail to promote these systems and teach them to others, your organization will become stagnant.

Most people start off using these systems but over time, they get bored with the process or let life get in the way and fail to follow up. It's true that systems can become boring or even monotonous, but network marketing is all about consistent, repetitive behavior, so rest assured that even if it feels stale, you're doing it right. Systems are meant to move in perfect precision, with what seems to be very little effort.

Though they may not be the most dynamic business methods in the world, systems can truly drive a business toward success. They are also helpful when it comes to other aspects of network marketing, including:

1. **Exponential duplication.** This is the compounded growth phenomenon that occurs in your organization. It's similar to the compound interest you may earn on money invested in a mutual fund or stock. Two people sponsoring two people each exponentially grows to six people total. Six

people sponsoring six more each exponentially grows to thirty-six. This is predicated on enough people doing their share of sponsoring, and is necessary in order to build a large organization rapidly.

2. **Train your organization properly.** Training can be called the "secret formula" in network marketing. When new people are sponsored into your organization, they have limited knowledge about the company, the product or service it offers, and the steps involved in getting started properly. Training is the bridge that can take your new recruits from amateur to professional—to the level where they can actually earn a living building their network marketing businesses. Professional network marketers have the ability to produce bigger, faster results by training team members in the areas of recruiting, marketing their services and teaching others to do the same.

3. **Tracking your business.** There is a philosophy in network marketing: You can't inspect what you don't inspect. This simply means that just like in any other business, you must track the activity and results of your network marketing business on a regular basis in order to reach your anticipated goals. Data has to be collected, such as how many people are added to your team each week as a result of the team's recruiting efforts. Knowing information such as how much product (or services) is sold weekly

within your group can become extremely valuable to your efforts to stay on track and meet your financial goals.

4. **Keeping your team plugged in and informed.** Communication is a key component of every successful organization. It is absolutely essential to have as much communication as possible with your organization, as often as possible. Let them know about meetings, trainings and special announcements from you or the company through e-mail blasts, calling post systems that call your entire organization, or any other communication system that is duplicatible.

5. **Creating accountability.** Remember, you are building a volunteer army of reps who don't have to do anything in their business. This is why it is up to you, as a leader, to create a voluntary system of accountability that will help you track and monitor the performance of your team. Through your leadership influence and example, people will voluntarily enroll into systems that you implement to help keep the team productive. These systems can be in the form of weekly activity reports or weekly calls with your top leaders to discuss what activities they engaged in, and their results.

Spencer's View

Avoid Building an Average Team

Even while I was growing up, I never wanted to be average. I wanted to make above-average grades, score above-average points on the basketball team and earn above-average money at my afterschool job. I guess you could say that I was a bit of an overachiever.

This is a common trait among The 3 CEOs and other highly successful people: We *expect* to win. Losing, or being average, is just not an option, no matter what the situation. If there's a recruit we have an eye on, we expect to sign them up. If there's a sales benchmark to meet, you bet that we aim to surpass it. Heck, if there's a door prize being raffled off and 20,000 names are in the pool, we're crazy enough to think that one of our names should be pulled—and will probably be upset if it isn't. Why? Because we expect to win. That's just how we are.

In your business and in your life, you must expect to win as well, and you must assemble a team that feels the same way, too. As you build your team, look for people who are frustrated with being average. They don't have to be arrogant; they just have to be confident in their skills, with the determination and desire to succeed where the average person will not. When you find a handful of people who think like this, your organization will grow like never before because people with this mindset often associate with or know others who think and respond the same way—providing a wide circle of potential representatives for your business.

People with the above-average mindset don't spend a lot of time with negative, low-energy people. Why not? Because they understand that a pessimistic attitude can become contagious; it can spread like a cancer throughout their organizations. People with the above-average mindset don't spend a lot of time complaining about things that they have no control over because they understand that it robs them of quality time that should be spent on improving the things over which they do have control.

In addition, people with an above-average mindset are

willing to do the things that average people will not in order to have things that the average person will not have. In other words, they pay the price to be successful. This often requires long hours on the road working with their organizations, long hours on the phone explaining the benefits of their opportunities, and time away from home and the ones they love the most. But guess what? It's tough becoming wealthy—just as tough as it is to be broke. So, if it's going to be hard either way, why not choose the wealthy option?

In Team Building, You Sometimes Have to Play Scrabble

Okay, so you've been working your business and have experienced some good growth. People are excited, and the checks are coming in pretty regularly. Life is good. But then, all of a sudden, your business just hits the wall. Nothing seems to work. The team that you relied on simply has stopped replicating your efforts and has instead begun to impact your earnings for the worse. What do you do?

Play Scrabble—the classic game where each player chooses seven random letters and tries to make words from them. When the game starts, it's pretty easy to make good words, but as the board becomes more crowded, the letters that you relied on earlier in the game no longer work for you. When this happens, the rules allow you to take a pass, exchange all seven pieces and pick new ones, which often results in a new configuration of words—and victory.

Similarly, in team building, sometimes you can't rely on the same old pieces—the recruits who helped you build momentum in the early stages of your business. As the network marketing playing field gets more crowded and the competition begins to intensify, you may have to forget about the old pieces, recruit seven new players and use their new energy and enthusiasm to win!

You can apply this Scrabble principle to your everyday life as well. If you hang around four broke people, there is a strong possibility that, sooner or later, you are going to be the fifth! You may need to dump those old pieces, change your circle and get back in the game. Find a group that can help you improve the quality of your own life. Get the idea?

Breathe Easy!

Every time you board an airplane, the flight attendants issue some pre-flight instructions regarding the safety features of the aircraft, the use of electronics and what to do in the event of an emergency. One of the instructions they give is about the oxygen masks that will deploy in case of cabin pressure loss. "Please make sure that you secure your own mask before assisting others," they always tell you.

How does this relate to network marketing? Well, it speaks to the importance of making sure that you have a solid foundation for yourself before you do anything else. If you don't have a solid foundation, anything you build upon it will crumble and fail in time, and in network marketing, that often means taking others down with you.

Unfortunately, people don't always realize this. They enjoy some small success in the beginning stages of their businesses and go on to make some pretty dramatic decisions, like quitting their jobs prematurely. We've seen people get started in networking and within their first thirty days, come to one of our meetings and exclaim, "I just fired my boss! I'm going to be a full-time network marketer!"

Sadly, their enthusiasm is misplaced. In reality, they didn't "fire their boss"; they quit their job and removed themselves from their only source of financial stability. Sustaining a full-time income in this industry is quite an accomplishment and very few are actually able to do it—that's the reality of network marketing.

With nothing to fall back on—with no solid foundation—people like this may soon be working their new networking opportunities under economic duress, and that's not good.

The decision to work a networking business full-time should not be taken lightly. You must give careful consideration to the sound advice of your leaders and mentors, and make sure that you have that good foundation in place. We recommend that you have at least one year's worth of cash savings in the bank before even considering such a risky move.

Don't Be a Sluggard

What is a "sluggard"? That's someone who is lazy, who just seems to have no sense of urgency about anything. In The 3 CEOs, all of us are just the opposite of sluggards; personally, I walk fast, I talk fast, I eat fast and I process information fast. I just can't seem to slow down—not necessarily a good trait in everyday life, but in business, it can certainly be an advantage.

Sluggards often sabotage their own success without even knowing it, just by not remembering to think ahead. Shopping in fine stores around the world, Floyd, Donald and I watch people spend hundreds and in some cases thousands of dollars in an instant, on useless items such as purses, sunglasses, video game consoles and so on. Then, when they are presented with an opportunity to invest in their futures and their own personal development, they suddenly don't have the money because they failed to plan ahead or simply don't see the need to become a merchant instead of a constant consumer.

Then, you have the group of people who insist—and almost brag—about how skeptical they are of everything and everyone. They think that they are smart, that they will keep themselves safe and secure because they don't really trust what anyone says. Well, to that, I say that skepticism is only valuable in the absence of logic. In other words, some things just make sense. People use the veil of skepticism to hide behind a myriad of excuses ranging from their own feelings of inadequacy and low self-esteem to past failures in business and a simple inability to admit that they don't have the money to invest in the opportunity at the time. But all they're doing is fooling themselves. It's okay to trust people; in fact, it's downright healthy. And if a person you trust comes to you with an opportunity to become financially free, why on earth would you not take it?

In business, you must seize the moment and outpace the competition. I tell my son, Brandon, that every day that he is not outside practicing his basketball drills, somewhere, someone else is. It's similar in business: For every day that you spend doing nothing to advance your position or increase your market share, the competition is getting ahead of you, and it won't be long before you get caught, passed and ultimately left behind.

"Pull the Trigger"

People often sit in their offices or cubicles at work and stare longingly out the window, or simply daydream about being somewhere else, living their dreams. Why are some people fulfilling their dreams in life while others are not? The answer is, often, that the successful person, at some point in his or her life, stopped *talking* about doing something different and *did something different*. We call this "pulling the trigger."

The idea is to stop sitting around the house, talking about losing weight, and pull the trigger—develop a plan and commit yourself to a regimen of healthy eating and exercise. Stop complaining about how stupid your boss is and pull the trigger—have the confidence to look for a position that will allow you to use your abilities and talents. Stop looking at the tropical island screensaver on your computer and pull the trigger—start saving for and planning your dream vacation.

The point is that you must do everything in your life with a sense of purpose and a sense of urgency. Otherwise, you'll look at yourself in the mirror one day and not recognize the aged face that's staring back at you!

You must also get accustomed to pulling the trigger in your business. Some people tell me that they plan on hosting a meeting "*next* month" or will call a few people about their business "*next* week." But procrastination like that will cause you to become the *next* network marketing casualty. Why? Because you will never develop or build momentum by putting off for tomorrow what you can do today. While you're waiting and waiting and waiting, your competition is talking to your friends, your minister, your girlfriend and everyone else you know, and getting them involved in a great opportunity—theirs, not yours.

Understand Your Business

There are three areas of the networking business that you must come to intimately know and understand:

- **The Product**. You must know what you are selling or representing. If it's a tangible good (i.e., a device, a nutritional supplement, a beverage, etc.), you must know its benefits and drawbacks. You should know and understand what makes your product unique, different and better than the competition. Know the answers to questions regarding price and availability.

  Also, be very careful of companies that offer "high-tech" products. We're living in an age when the computer you bought thirty days ago is just about obsolete today. Change is happening rapidly; companies whose main products hinge on new technology often do not survive for the long-term because it's just a matter of time until something better, faster and cheaper comes along.

If your opportunity is service-oriented (i.e., financial, legal, travel, etc.), study the trends that are appropriate to the service's industry. Use Google to find pertinent, *objective* information about it on the Internet. We stress objectivity because simply studying a company's internal marketing material and propaganda is *subjective*—that is, based on the opinions and views of the people who run the company themselves. A company's marketing material will always slant toward the positive, beneficial aspects of their products and services, and you need to read something that will not.

No matter how well-read you are, though, don't make the mistake of thinking that people are stupid. Your potential customers will have access to the same information online and will often come to a presentation more informed about your industry than you are. Be sure to look at your business from all perspectives from the beginning, so that you can gain a complete picture of what it does and what it sells.

- **The Plan.** This is big. Study your company's compensation plan and ask questions. Is it a binary plan? Is it a true multi-level matrix or simply single-level residuals? Are there charge-backs? Are there any quotas that you must meet or minimum monthly purchases required?

I learned a long time ago that the only stupid questions are the ones not asked, and I can't stress enough what an important concept this is. Think of it this way: When you're interviewing for a job, you ask tons of questions before you accept the position. You want to know what the sick-day policy is, what type of benefits are offered and what will be expected of you from day to day— and, you definitely would not accept a job without understanding *how you get paid!*

This is the approach you should take when evaluating opportunities in network marketing. Not asking these questions could cause you to spend your hard-earned money on a program that probably wasn't right for you from the beginning.

- **The People.** Study this area from two perspectives. First, look at the company's owners or founders. Remember, success leaves clues—*but so does failure.* In every opportunity, trace the roots back to the founders and ask questions like, "What is their track record in business?" "Is this the first time they've started a business like this?" and "What is their reputation?"

The answers to questions like this are vitally important to the long-term success of a company. Floyd, Donald and I have been blessed to work with a company whose founders have a stellar track record. They have a long history of success spanning more than forty years; they've earned tens of millions of dollars in the same industry over time; and, most importantly, they are God-fearing, ethical businessmen with an impeccable reputation both in and out of the networking community. When we were considering joining, all of this gave us the reassurance we needed that this company would be around for quite some time.

Second, you must look at the company's customer base and examine the needs and spending habits of the people who will be joining your program or purchasing your products or services. Once again, under-standing this component will dictate whether or not the program is right for you. You should choose a program that suits not just you but also the people in your circle of influence, since they may be joining your business in the future.

Donald's View

Keeping Focus

In network marketing, it's all about the team. Without yours, you'd be nothing—you'd never sell much product, and your business, in a word, would fail. This industry hinges on the power of people working together and the more of them you can get together to work toward that ultimate goal—financial freedom—the better.

Although, as Floyd and Spencer have already emphasized, it's not exactly the number of people on your team that's important—it's how good they are at doing what they do. Having an enormous team is, of course, a great goal to have, but if you're employing thousands of people who are only mediocre at best, where is the advantage in that? The key is to recruit smart; don't just invite every person you meet. You have to really get to know who you're working with—know their strengths, their weaknesses and what you can do to help them improve on both.

And how can you do this? By focusing—on each person individually, on their talents and skills, and on what they can do for the team as a whole. While many network marketers look to increase the sizes of their teams by twenty or thirty at a time, The 3 CEOs method is to build a team one person at a time. This means that I may not bring in 100 people myself, but I *will* bring in three qualified, talented people who in turn will bring in 3,000.

An analogy I like to use to illustrate this point is, believe it nor not, having a baby. Whether you're a woman or a man, try to imagine what it would be like to go into a hospital expecting to give birth to one son or daughter—and coming out with ten. Even though you hadn't planned on or prepared for having that many children, you have to take them home with you, and do the best you can to care for them with whatever resources you have. Each of these new lives will have special needs, and you must see to them all, at the same time, without missing a beat. If you're distracted for even a moment, those who you are not paying attention to will be off doing their own thing in no time, and probably getting into some trouble.

Can you see how this relates to running a large team? When you have a group of, say, a thousand people who are not all entirely focused on the same goal, it can become difficult, as their leader, to keep them in line. You will have to put in more time and expend more energy just to keep them all focused on the goal, and thus have less time yourself to run the business and enjoy the rewards. Really, when you recruit for numbers instead of talent, you are only making more work for yourself.

And if you don't have the time to "babysit" the people on your team who need it, and keep an eye on all they do, some of them may wander off—which means not working to the best of their ability, not doing the work they are supposed to or in any way, not supporting the team's efforts. Members like this can really bring a team down and affect your bottom line. Can your business afford such a drain on its profits?

When you bring in one person at a time, however, this is rarely a problem. Because you have taken the time to know a person—and his or her skill set—before bringing them onboard, it will be easier to get them "up and running" as far as the business goes. This is what we mean when we talk about leaders training leaders: You want to bring in that one person or those two people who, like yourself, will be capable of taking the ball and running with it—in other words, spending some time in training to get up to speed with the specifics of the business, then just going out there and starting to do it, no "babysitting" required.

Coachable Members Make Credible Leaders
One important thing to keep in mind while building your team one member at a time is that everyone comes into network marketing at a different phase of personal development. Some are older, some are younger; some have twenty years' experience in corporate America, some have only a few. Some prospective team members and future leaders will be able to jump right into the work and become leaders in their own right almost immediately. Some will need a little bit of coaching to bring them up to speed.

As their leader, it is your responsibility to recognize these differences and act on them. In my view, there is no generic training method when it comes to network marketing. Instead, you must be ready to offer more personalized, hands-on, one-to-one mentoring, especially to those who need more guidance. Not everyone is born with all the skills they'll need to be great leaders themselves, but they can, through personal development and their leaders' help, acquire them.

Of course, they have to keep in mind that being mentored is a two-way street. They must actively participate in their coaching, and take advantage of what their leader—most likely, a seasoned, successful professional in the industry—has to say. One of the most important skills that a successful future leader must develop within him-or herself is the ability to be coachable, or the ability to work with the person who wants to tell them how to succeed.

This was how I started out in network marketing. I knew nothing about the industry at the time; I was just busy working my nine-to-five job, paying my bills and trying to get by. But of course, like everyone else, I was also on the lookout for something better.

Then I met a gentleman who introduced me to a networking opportunity. He pointed out that I traveled for business anyway—so why shouldn't I join a travel business, and make some money from my efforts? It made sense, and this man seemed credible to me—a very important factor when you're trying to recruit new team members. If you don't give off an air of believability—and have the accomplishments to back it up—no one will want to get in on what you're doing. Do you think that you have enough credibility to make others believe in what you have to offer? Others will be able to tell by the way in which you interact with the people around you. Do people listen to you, and respond to what you tell them? Are they interested in your ideas? If they are, this speaks of a history of good performance; you've already shown these people that you are smart, reliable and innovative, and so they are willing to listen to whatever new thoughts you might have.

And that was how this gentleman seemed to me. I saw him talking to other people, and he seemed very well-received. He was well-spoken, nicely dressed and not at all pushy about what he had to say. And what he said made sense. He was showing me how *I* could benefit from this network marketing opportunity— not how *he* could benefit from my joining. He was interested in my life, my interests and my skills, and based on all this, I signed up before his presentation had even begun.

This is a great approach to take when you're out there meeting people and trying to find some new leaders for your team. How the opportunity is introduced will determine how it is perceived, so you want to make sure that you sound just as honest, hard-working and intelligent as you actually are. Pay attention to how you look and what you say, as well as how you listen. Nothing turns people off faster than the perception that they are not being heard; if your potential recruit senses that while you're talking to them, you're thinking about the next pitch you're going to give them, well, that's a sure-fire way to turn them off to the idea real fast. And that's a shame, because that could have just been your next best leader.

Today, the man who introduced me to my first network marketing opportunity is already retired, and that says a lot about how he ran his business. While recruiting, he talked the talk and with his team, he walked the walk. As a leader, you have to not just say what people want to hear, but what they need to hear— including, sometimes, that an opportunity is not for them. By "weeding out" those who are not ready for network marketing yet, or those who are not really interested, you will make room for those who *are* interested, and those who are ready for financial freedom.

Which brings us back to coachability. This is one of the most important characteristics that you can look for in a new team member. When I first started out, as I said earlier, I had little idea what network marketing was about, but I wanted to learn. I wanted to find out how I could become financially free, and was willing to do the work it might take me to get there. When I signed up, I was in essence saying to the leader, "Teach me everything you know!" He did, and together, we found success. To this day, I keep that open-minded attitude toward learning, and my achievements continue to grow.

Setting Small Goals

The objective in network marketing is to build a championship team—one that will do whatever it takes to reach its goals.

The key is not to set one overall goal for everyone, as that would be unrealistic. We are all individuals, after all, with our own thoughts, opinions, desires and needs. Instead, as the leader, you need to set up a series of small, more easily achievable goals that when taken as a whole, add up to the big picture for which you're aiming.

As an example, when Michael Jordan came into the NBA, he said that he would score thirty-two points in one game. Seems like a lot, doesn't it? I can just imagine what it would feel like, trying for those baskets and keeping an eye on the clock, minutes ticking down as the total slowly, slowly made its way to thirty-two.

But Michael, as smart as he was, broke it down instead. He took those thirty-two points he promised and looked at it as just eight points per quarter, a much more workable number. It also gave him a chance, at the end of each quarter, to review his results and change his strategy, if necessary, to make it to the points he wanted to reach.

With your team in network marketing, you should adopt a similar way of doing things. You could just say, "Our goal is to be financially free," and that would be true, and something to work toward. But how would you do it? What steps would you take to be financially free? What would it take for you and your team to get to that place, and how long?

These are a lot of questions to answer—too many, when you're trying to run a team. Although you should have at least one overarching goal for yourself, your team and your business in general, to get to that goal, you have to start small. Set daily goals first—goals that will produce quicker results while at the same time adding to the greater good. That is, you want to always do things that will push you a step further toward your target, while at the same time giving you a sense of accomplishment— a powerful tool when it comes to motivation.

The advantage of this, as noted in the Michael Jordan example, is that smaller goals give you a chance to reflect on your work and its results, and make changes to your course of action if necessary, and all before things go too far south. If there's a wrench in the works, it's better to find out as soon as possible, and get it out of there before you're nearly at your goal, when you'll have so much more to lose.

Sacrifice

Anyone who has owned a business before knows how much sacrifice is involved. Your energy, your money, time with your family and loved ones—all of it, at some point, takes a backseat to the business you're trying to run. It will not last forever—there will come a time when you'll be able to sit back and enjoy the rewards of your hard work—but it's a fact of life that if you want to "be your own boss," there will be a period of just making ends meet.

In network marketing, I've made that sacrifice, as have the rest of The 3 CEOs. We've all put in our time and our money, and had some pretty lean years to show for it. The key is consistency and persistence; in other words, keep doing what you're doing and eventually, it's going to pay off.

What we've found from our experiences in the industry, actually, is that success goes hand in hand with sacrifice. If you are not willing to give up a little of your own personal comfort and security, then you are not going to be able to eventually achieve the goals you set out for yourself. Unfortunately, this is how so many people think; they spend the better parts of their lives working at jobs where they build other people's corporations and make other people rich, but aren't willing to put the same time and effort into doing those things for themselves.

I understand this, to an extent. It's hard to give up the security of a weekly paycheck and go into business for yourself. It takes a lot of courage and a lot of work, and some people just aren't in the right situation to give up that steady flow of income at the moment when they're approached with an opportunity.

That's okay; as I said earlier, everyone enters network marketing at their own stage of personal development. Maybe some just aren't ready to enter it yet at all, but that doesn't mean that they never will be. They just have to wait until the time is right—until they can make the sacrifice that will be necessary to get things moving.

In this business, you get out what you put in. If all you can give to your network marketing business is, say, ten percent of your time, then things are not going to move very quickly. As we've stated over and over, network marketing is not a get-rich-quick scheme; it's a legitimate business with all the trappings of the real thing. And, as with any other type of business, if you try to do it part-time, then you will have part-time results. To make your way toward real financial freedom, you may have to give up some freedom along the way, but in the end, you will be paid back for that time, money and effort exponentially. You just have to stick with it, and never give up on your goal.

SIDE THREE
DRIVEN FROM WITHIN

Floyd's View

Work Ethic and Drive

A solid work ethic is all about stamina, focus and consistency. It has to do with not just doing your job but doing it to the best of your ability and then some, about staying with it when things are rough, and about having the determination and tenacity to succeed.

Networking is a long-term venture that calls for an exceptional work ethic and a commitment of continuous drive. As The 3 CEOs, Spencer, Donald and I are intrinsically driven from within to succeed; our individual work ethics drive us to do whatever it takes to achieve our goals. But where does this drive come from? Can it be acquired or manufactured? Or is it something with which you just have to be born?

Personally, I think that a good work ethic is something that must be instilled in you at a young age. Though I primarily credit my work ethic and drive to my parents, I can trace them all the way back to my great-grandmother—an interesting character, to say the least. She ran a café inside a run-down little shack. She served hot, fried fish and grits; there was also a little music for the customers to enjoy, as well as some gambling and a whole lot of whisky. In the Deep South, fine establishments such as this were called "juke joints"—little holes in the wall where common folk could go for entertainment. It was a normal occurrence for someone to get beat up or even cut up in juke joints like the one my great-grandma ran. That was just the kind of places they were.

Great-Grandma's café was closed and boarded up by the time I was born, but my mother used to tell me stories of when she worked in the kitchen as a little girl, and I do recall the times my brother and I spent at Great-Grandma's house in the later years of her life. Even in her seventies, she continued to run a little business in the kitchen of her three-room rowhouse. She would sell fish sandwiches and shot glasses of whisky for fifty cents apiece— that's right, my great-grandma was a moonshiner! Okay, well, not exactly. She didn't make the moonshine herself. She was more of a repackager and reseller of fine spirits.

When my brother and I stayed with her on occasion, she would not allow us to go into the kitchen when customers were around. Wait, did I say "customers"? Actually, they would be better described as hobos and bums. My great-grandmother affectionately called them the "riff-raff of society"; they all kind of resembled Otis, from Mayberry, who got toasted all the time then went to the jailhouse himself to let Andy Griffith arrest him.

As little boys, my brother and I would peep in from the adjoining room to observe my great-grandma's operation. Old, beat-up and run-down fellas would come in through the back door, sit down and order a shot glass of liquor. Some would come back four or five times in one day, fifty cents in hand every time. They would have done better to go directly to the liquor store themselves and purchase the entire bottle. The only problem was that they didn't have a way to get to the store—nor did they have enough to pay for a whole bottle. By watching how my great-grandma made her profits, I learned two important rules of running a successful business: First, location is everything and second, pay attention to supply and demand.

Though it may have seemed like a casual way to make some extra money, my great–grandma's business was for real, and she had a whole set of rules to go along with it. She had a system in running her home-based business:

1. There was a three-drink maximum per visit, to keep customers from getting worked up.

2. It was cash only, no credit.

3. No cursing.

4. Only one customer could enter at a time.

And most people stuck to these guidelines. My great-grandma was a tough woman. Rarely did anyone try to cross her.

Every now and then, though, someone would break the rules and have to be reminded. I remember one regular customer named Little Willie, who came in quite often. One day, Little Willie staggered in, sat down and ordered a shot of whisky—and then another, and then a third. Little Willie was feeling pretty good, and he began talking loudly. Then, he let out a curse word.

"Okay, Little Willie, that's it. You've got to go," my great-grandma said. "You know I don't allow no cursin' in my place!"

Little Willie just sat there, sipping the last drop of his whisky.

"I ain't ready to go," he said in reply. "I ain't finished with my—"

Whack! Before Little Willie could get the last words out of his mouth, my great-grandma had smacked him in the middle of his shoulder blades with her walking stick.

"Ouch, Miss Lossie!" he shouted. "You didn't have to hit me with that stick. I was going!"

Great-Grandma glared at him. "You better be going!" she yelled back.

My brother and I looked at each other in fear and amazement. "Wow," I said. "Now I know why Great-Grandma calls that her walking stick. If you see her reach for it, you'd better be walking!"

Usually, that was all it took to straighten someone out who had a problem understanding my great-grandma's rules. And I knew if that walking stick didn't work, the pistol she carried in her apron would surely do the trick.

Though I never condoned my great-grandma's illegal enterprise, it was her way of maintaining her independence. She was determined—driven, even—not to rely on welfare or other people for her livelihood. You could say that in her own way, she wanted to be financially free. Maybe she didn't aspire to making millions, but she did want to earn her own money and use it as she pleased. And she knew that to have that privilege, she had to work for it. These were the lessons I learned from her.

Like my great-grandma, my parents worked hard all their lives, and they taught my brothers and me to do the same. Both my father and mother worked the same full-time jobs for over twenty years, with part-time jobs on the side as well. What drove them to succeed? Where did their work ethic originate? First and foremost, from the responsibility of family. They were driven to take care of my brothers and me, and to allow us the opportunity to go to college. They accomplished those goals through commitment to a continuous work ethic. In other words, they knew they had to work for it, and they did so every day that they could. I couldn't have asked for better role models during my formative years.

I have used the lessons that my parents taught me about consistent work ethic to succeed in many areas of my life. I got my first job at the age of nine—one summer, my brother and I worked a few days a week in a flower nursery. For a kid my age, it was pretty hard work, but we didn't miss a day of it, mostly because we liked the money but also because we discovered that hard work created a great sense of self-worth, and I had never slept better in my life.

Later, my work ethic helped me excel in athletics. As a young kid, I always played sports and because of the drive my parents had instilled in me, I excelled in everything I tried. I never missed team practices and always worked on my skills on my own. As a youth, my work ethic allowed me to lead my basketball teams to championships, and I was chosen as most valuable player more than once.

In high school, my basketball skills developed even further, and I was chosen to represent the entire league on the all-star team—and all because I had cultivated my God-given skills and a consistent work ethic. I was not a six-foot-five prototypical basketball player; at 5'10", I always had to prove to people that I was exceptional. Now, you'd think that would have bothered me, but it didn't. As a matter of fact, I used the challenge as a source of motivation. To prove that I was good enough, or even better than the rest, I would just go out on the court and wreak havoc on my opponent. It didn't take long for everyone to see that I was the real deal!

They say that sports are a good analogy for life, and having created my own success in high school athletics, I can attest that this old adage is true. Because I didn't look a certain way, coaches and even my fellow players never thought that I would amount to much, but strictly based on my own determination, I proved them wrong. Similarly, throughout your life, people will attempt to downplay your ability to achieve great things just because you are new to the business, or because they don't believe in what you're doing. My advice: Just look forward to the looks on their faces when you wave to them from the top! Hold on to that champion attitude and, above all, your solid work ethic, and even when things are challenging, they will take you wherever you need to go.

Why Build With Urgency?

My colleagues in The 3 CEOs, Spencer Iverson and Donald Bradley, are men of many talents—too many to list right here and now. But I would like to look at one of Donald's greatest attributes, one that has brought him and his team much success in network marketing: the ability to understand that in order to create momentum, you have to build with a sense of urgency.

What does this mean? Building with urgency means forming your team not as fast as you can, but as efficiently and productively as possible. Donald constantly motivates the rest of us to keep it moving, to keep getting out there, talking to people and bringing in the best people we can find. Underlying this is his great understanding that in business, you can't wait for things to happen; you simply have to make things happen for yourself.

And you can do this by having that sense of urgency. The philosophy that Donald shares with us all is "let's do it now," and that's a mantra that we in turn try to pass on to our team leaders. Yes, it is true what Abraham Lincoln said: "Good things come to those who wait." But I think that he could have also added more to that quote—something like, "But those who wait get the leftovers of those who hustled."

One of the problems that some people in network marketing find when trying to retain that sense of urgency is that networking has no deadline when it comes to success. Generally speaking, for most people, success in this industry is not a sprint but a marathon; as we've mentioned numerous times already, to get the rewards, you have to put in the time. Overnight success stories are few and far between. You will more than likely spend a few years working toward your own financial freedom in network marketing.

So while working with a sense of urgency may not make your success come any faster, it *will* make a difference in the *level* of success you enjoy. Typically, people who get off to a fast start and continue to maintain a sense of urgency end up becoming the top income earners in their company. How does this happen? It's a phenomenon that I can explain with a simple illustration.

Imagine rolling a 100-pound ball down a football field. If you relied on your own ability, and exerted minimal energy to push the ball, you could probably get to the end of the football field at some point in time. The process would be very painful, exhaustive and unpleasant, but you could do it.

On the other hand, what if you used the power of velocity and leverage? If you quickly recruited five qualified people to help you roll this huge ball—five strong individuals who were prepared for the task—before you exerted much of your own energy, you could, together, exert *maximum* energy and push with much more force. This creates momentum against the resistance of the heavy ball, and makes it roll faster toward its target.

Now, why are these people helping you move this ball? Because it's a challenge, and that's what drives them. Self-motivation like this is a key quality to look for in potential team members; you don't want people who will put their hands on the ball and pretend to make an effort, but those who push with urgency and quickness to get it done.

With all of you pushing at once, the ball will pick up so much speed that it will seem as if it's rolling on its own. When this happens, no one person can take responsibility for the speed at which it moves—it's teamwork, plain and simple.

As you move down the field, that incredible momentum will create excitement for any onlookers who happen to be around, and undoubtedly they will want to be a part of what's going on. They may run out on the field, just to get their hands on the ball of energy; most of them won't know where the ball is going exactly, but they will want to be there when it arrives.

With all of this support around you, the ball will keep rolling toward the goal at blazing speed. You won't feel tired; you won't even be concerned when some people take their hands off the ball, because the goal will be within your sight. Then, all of a sudden, you'll be there. Is that exhilarating or what?

There are many things to learn from this example of urgency, teamwork and motivation:

- Reserve your individual energy and stamina. You'll need it to go the complete distance.
- Recruiting qualified partners to help you creates powerful leverage and makes difficult tasks a lot easier—and even enjoyable.
- Your mental and emotional attitude has to be positive, enthusiastic and confident as you experience faster and easier results.
- Immediately surrounding yourself with people who have the same goals and objectives as you can really be energizing. Their strength enhances your ability and keeps you striving for that continually raising bar.

That's the power of building with urgency, and there is no better way to improve your odds of becoming successful in network marketing. Yes, building a network marketing business slowly is possible, but it's like pushing that 100-pound ball up the hill yourself. Most people who attempt this method get winded in the process; they build slowly, enroll a few people from time to time who are only putting their hands on the ball with no commitment, and never get enough momentum to make a significant impact. They never get enough qualified, committed people at one time to get that maximum effort.

What Is Your Why?

Having a big "why"—a big reason for doing what you do—is critical in creating a work ethic and keeping yourself committed to the business. Your "why" can be anything from taking care of your children to attaining financial freedom for just yourself, though, typically, your "why" must be bigger than just making a lot of money.

Over the years, I've had a list of reasons why working my network marketing business was important, and why I absolutely needed to be successful. I wrote them all down in the journals that I kept; here is a list that was recorded over six years ago:

My "Why"
- Great education for my children
- Self-worth
- Making our home nice for my wife
- Not being worried about finances
- Having good transportation for my wife and myself
- Being able to buy my mother a new car
- Getting fit and staying healthy

Recently, when I reviewed this list of goals, I was shocked and amazed: I had already accomplished each and every one of them. Today, my son, Jordan, goes to one of the finest private schools in Georgia. My daughter, Carmen, graduated from the same school and now attends one of the most prestigious universities in the country. My wife, Carla, and I have been able to build our dream home, including a gym to keep me healthy and fit; we not only have good transportation, but we both own luxury vehicles. And I was able to buy my mother a brand-new car.

Money has not been a problem for a long time for me and my family. More importantly, all this has given me a sense of self-worth that I have never experienced before. Through creating my "big why" list and committing myself to attaining every item on it, I learned first-hand what a powerful exercise goal-setting can be. It teaches you discipline, and really puts your work ethic to the test.

So, what do you do when you accomplish all the things on your "why" list? That' easy: You find another "why." The success that I have experienced in network marketing is still remarkable to me, and has allowed me to accomplish almost all of my material "whys." Although I remain truly thankful to God for the cars, the homes and the lifestyle my family and I have been afforded, it is no longer the "why" that drives me to outwork other people in the industry. The novelty of all the "stuff" begins to wear off after a while, like the smell of a new car fading after you take it home.

The one thing that success in network marketing has afforded me that I never will get used to, the one thing that never grows old, is the ability to wake up every morning with total freedom to decide what I want to do. The feeling of not having anyone in my life dictating where I have to be and what time I need to get there is amazing. For me, that feeling is priceless, and I never want to give it up. Making sure that freedom is protected is what drives me today, and is my biggest "why" for working hard in this industry.

Keeping It Moving Through the Challenges
Some years ago, my family and I fell on some very difficult times financially. As a result of a series of unfortunate events, my small ad agency, which had been very successful for ten years, closed

its doors. That was one of the most challenging times of my life. We literally just ran out of money. I remember driving home, pulling into my driveway and just sitting in the car, staring into space. My eyes began to well up with tears as I contemplated the possibility of having to file for bankruptcy. With all that I had accomplished, and all I had to give up, I felt like a complete failure.

Every afternoon, it was the same routine. The phone constantly rang with calls from creditors, demanding what Carla and I did not have. "Mr. Williams," they'd say, "your account is ninety days past due, plus late fees and over-the-limit fees. We need you to make a payment today." To that, all I could say was, "You're on the list, with all the others." There were so many creditors calling that neither Carla nor I wanted to answer the phone.

I was embarrassed and ashamed of where I was in life. Every day, I asked myself, "How did I get here? I'm just a respectable, honest person who wants to take care of my family and pay my bills." I thought on it and thought on it, and still, no answers came to me—and no relief from the overwhelming stress of a life in disarray.

As far as earning a living, I had retained a few of my advertising clients and still had projects to do for them, but it wasn't generating enough income to maintain our household, even with Carla working hard in corporate America. I eventually went out to search for a position with a larger ad agency, but even then, the salaries I was offered were not enough to take care of our monthly obligations.

So, I decided to work full-time and take a part-time position as well. I would work in advertising during the day and head out to my part-time job at midnight; I would drive twenty-five miles to an old warehouse on the outskirts of town to work through the night rolling newspapers, stuffing them into plastic bags and delivering them to customers. I was a college graduate, a big ad man, in a warehouse filled with folks who probably never even graduated from high school: people whom society looked down on, people of no perceived value.

And they were also the people who were now telling me what to do. Despite my education and my former career, I still had to get the warehouse manager's permission to take a break and follow whatever newspaper rolling and stuffing quotas he set for me. My life, I felt, had sunk to an all-time low; it was a humbling experience, to say the least. But I stuck with it, because I needed the money.

In fact, for the next year and a half, I worked part-time jobs like this one just to help make ends meet. I will never forget working as a bill collector for a major agency in Atlanta. What cruel irony! I sat in a little cubicle, calling people who were in the exact same situation that I was and asking them to pay their debts. I was supervised by people much younger than I was; they told me to make more calls faster, and to be sterner with people, or even to curse them out when necessary. I never took their advice or their approach to collecting money.

Despite that, I soon realized that I had a knack for getting people to give me payments over the phone. I believe that I was successful at that job because I was able to relate to where these people were in life—because I was exactly where they were. I remember one day when I came in to work as usual, ready to call the queue of phone numbers I had been assigned. I began to work the list, making each call, requesting payments and then tabbing down to the next name. After a few calls, I looked at the computer screen for the next name on the list and was shocked to find that it was my own. I was horrified. I didn't know what to do. So, I simply called myself and left a message. Needless to say, I didn't get a call back, and I did not collect a phone payment.

But like I said, extenuating circumstances aside, I was always able to get people to make their payments. Perhaps they could sense my sincerity and my genuine concern for them. I spoke to all my "clients" with compassion, while at the same time maintaining my objective, which was to get them to make an effort toward meeting their financial obligations. Many times, it was difficult, and some of those phone calls were not pleasant. I was hung up on, threatened and even cursed out a few times.

I remember calling a gentleman one evening, and he began to immediately light into me. He cursed me out and called me every name he could think of. I listened patiently, and did not interrupt him. I then responded to him in the most respectful and compassionate tone that I could muster. This man had said everything to me that I had wanted to say to all of those ignorant creditors who had bullied and harassed me for over a year. I understood where he was coming from, his frustration, and I felt compelled to speak to him with all the compassion and understanding that I would have loved to have received when I was on the other end of those phone calls. As I spoke to him, I could sense his frustration and anger melting away. He apologized for his behavior, and we began to have real dialogue. Before I got off the phone, he gave me a payment and made a future commitment toward his debt obligation.

I eventually became the number-one part-time collector in my department. The people I called almost always wanted to work with me to get their debt paid. I connected with them on a real level because I could literally feel their pain, and I know this made all the difference in meeting my goals.

While I was going through all of these challenges, it became difficult to envision life having more for me than just years of frustration and struggle. But later, I realized that all of those hard times were God's way of preparing me for the incredible blessings He would later bestow upon my family and me. He used those trials as a test to ensure that I would always remain humble and never look down upon anyone—unless I was attempting to help them up. Today, I am grateful to God for those trials, because they made me a better person.

A year after losing my business, I decided to change my career path because my "why"—getting my freedom back—had become more urgent than ever. I had lost the freedom that I'd had when I'd worked for myself; I'd gotten used to setting my own schedule and calling my own shots, and I wanted it to be that way again. But I knew that I had to take it one step at a time, and first work to stabilize my family's financial situation.

Carla was working her corporate job and making a great contribution to our family economy, but I always felt as though our financial welfare was primarily my responsibility. So, I decided to make a career change. I began researching the mortgage industry and decided that I would go to work for a company that would train me to be a loan officer. But, there was one slight challenge with this: There was no salary involved. Loan officers worked on commission only. Still, it was what I wanted to do.

Carla was not amused when I told her about it. There would be two months of training with absolutely no compensation, and she simply could not see it—but I could see it clearly. This would be the vehicle that would eventually allow both of us to experience the financial and temporal freedom I so desperately desired. This was, in my mind, the vehicle I would use to realize my one big "WHY."

So I accepted a position with a national mortgage company. It was a struggle for us financially, and the process was not a smooth one, to say the least. For months, I would get to the office at 8:00 a.m. and get home around nine at night, having earned not one penny. To be honest, once I'd started, I did want to quit, but I knew that giving up had never been the answer for me. I was not a quitter, and never respected people who quit when things got tough. I believed that if I just kept pounding away at it, life would have to give me what I demanded.

To strengthen my motivation, I began to call upon the things that I had learned over the years, while on my journey of personal development. Mental toughness and focus were important, and even necessary for me to keep going. I had invested a lot of time in acquiring skills that I now needed to utilize. I found that the Bible was the best source for direction and inspiration for me, as well as books like *Think and Grow Rich* by Napoleon Hill, *The Richest Man in Babylon* by George S. Clasen and *The Strangest Secret* by Earl Nightingale. I read, I studied, and I put everything I learned to work for me in one way or another. I might not have been making any money, but at least I was learning a lot.

Sure enough, things began to come together. Eventually, I became the number-one loan officer in the company and, later, I was appointed manager of the entire region. I'd gone from making nothing to earning more money than I had ever made working for any other company. Carla was even able to quit her job and be a stay-at-home mom. I was thrilled—the first phase of my plan was working. I was close to achieving that all-important "why."

But one half of it—the freedom of time—continued to elude me. Running a branch of a national company was extremely stressful and I found I was spending all my time just keeping up with it. The company I worked for owned me. My managers had to know what time I went to lunch, where I went and practically what I ate. They gave me a beeper so they could keep track of me 24/7. In time, I had given up all of my freedom, and practically my life, in exchange for a paycheck. I had no time to spend with my family, and I rarely saw my daughter, who was asleep when I left for work *and* when I got home at night. This was what I hated the most.

It all came to a head when my father took very ill after having a heart attack. He lived in South Carolina, and I was in Atlanta, Georgia. My parents had divorced during my second year in college and my father had lived by himself. When he became ill, he moved in with relatives.

I seldom had the luxury of taking time to drive to South Carolina to see my father. I would try to sneak out of town on a weekend when possible, but many times, I had to work on Saturdays and just couldn't get away. My father eventually suffered a stroke, and I brought him to live with us until he and I both realized that my wife and I were not capable of providing him with the 'round-the-clock attention he needed. He eventually went back to South Carolina, and I was able to hire a caretaker to be with him at all times.

There were days when I simply needed to take time off to help my dad take care of his affairs, but the demands of the people I reported to at work simply would not allow it. When I did get the time to go check on him, I'd find that the caretaker wasn't doing a very good job of attending to him; I'd have to get him out of bed, clean him up and change him like a baby because he had become almost helpless. This is one of the most painful memories that I have of my father.

Throughout this situation, I felt frustrated and helpless, mostly because I could not dictate how much time I could spend with him. I always had to get back to the job—it all came back to that. Never before in my life had my "why" about controlling my time seemed so important.

My father suffered another stroke in time and had to be hospitalized for almost a month. One night, a doctor called me from the hospital and told me to come as soon as possible because he didn't think that my father would make it through the night.

Without even once thinking of my all-important job, I immediately jumped in my car and set out on the longest drive of my life. During those lonely, uninterrupted hours on the road to South Carolina, I had time to reflect on my life, as well as on life in general. I wondered if I had made a good trade, or even a fair trade, in the career I'd pursued. Was it a good decision to exchange my life, my freedom and time with my family for a sense of financial stability?

The more I thought about it, the more I began to understand how short life is—in fact, I began to *feel* how short it is. And the further away from work I got, the less important it seemed. I hadn't brought along my pager, which I was supposed to have on me at all times, per my boss' instructions. I hadn't even bothered to contact him, to tell him where I would be. I simply did not care about him, his company or its rules. My father was dying that night, and nothing mattered other than that.

When I arrived at the hospital, nobody was there with my father. My two brothers had been contacted and were on their way from Maryland, but they would not arrive until the next morning. I will never forget going into that room and seeing Dad in intensive care; I still remember his distinctive breathing pattern, which doctors refer to as the "death rattle." It's an indication that the end of life is quickly approaching.

I held my father's hand and spoke to him clearly and calmly, without tears. I had cried for him often during his declining health; I had cried for him all during that long drive from Atlanta. Now, I knew that the present quality of his life was not something he would want to hold on to.

As I just stood there holding his cold hand, a calm came over me, a sense of peace that only God could give. I felt as though my father knew that I was there, even though he was unconscious. I could really feel his awareness. It was a beautiful moment between my dad and me, even though no words were spoken by either of us.

I spent that entire night at the hospital, and my dad hung on. Early the next morning, my older brother, Tim, arrived; my younger brother, Dennis, came soon after. Dennis really took it hard, and we simply allowed him to have his moment with my dad, as I had done the night before. I believe now that Dad had been hanging on long enough for Dennis to get to the hospital.

Tim and I went down to the cafeteria then, to shed some tears and talk about the memories we had of our father. When we went back to the room, we found Dennis and some other family members—our mother, and several of Dad's sisters—being ushered out into the hallway. Dad, it seemed, had taken his last breath. It was time for the medical staff to take care of his body.

On that day, at that moment, my "why" not only became bigger—it became a guarantee. I made a commitment that I would become so financially successful, no one would ever control my time and life again. I set a goal to ensure that my mother would never have to do what my father had done: work himself right into a heart attack and then a stroke. He had made the normal trade, the one we all make—his health and his freedom for the empty promise of the financial stability of a job. I also made a goal of not working myself to death just trying to make a living. This was, is and will be my biggest "why" for the rest of my life: the freedom to fully *live* my life.

Every time I think about my "why," I get emotional, and perhaps you can see why. Do your "whys" make you feel this way? Are they strong enough, and big enough, to make you shed some tears? Are they huge enough to drive you with relentless, unyielding determination?

If you don't have at least one "why" that you're passionate about, you'll have difficulty experiencing the success you're working. Your one passionate "why" will override any obstacle, opposition or setback that you will experience in your journey to the top. It will be the thing that impels you toward success.

So many people quickly abandon their network marketing businesses because their "whys" are simply not big enough. Without those strong, emotional goals in mind, those reasons why they work as hard as they do, they have no motivation to push themselves toward success. There isn't enough at stake to make them care and, hence, their businesses suffer.

After my father passed away, I went back to my job physically, but emotionally, I had already left the building. Although I continued to do my job well, I was making plans to start my own mortgage company and entertaining thoughts of working my network marketing business again. A year later, I had opened my own mortgage office with one of my former employees, and had the time for networking, along with my wife, as well. It took only eleven months for us to reach the top level of the company.

At that point, I turned my half of the mortgage business over to my partner, as Carla and I had both decided to go full-time with the network marketing company and make my "why," finally, into reality. We worked with that company full-time for almost five years, continuing to learn and grow the entire time through the personal development that network marketing affords. In those years, we learned how to become leaders and, more importantly, how to create leaders .

Over the next several years, my "why" would be the fuel that allowed us to go straight to the top of several network marketing companies. Today, our "why" continues to be a solid and wonderful reality. We have been on an incredible journey, and we only have God to thank for that.

If you truly desire to be successful in this industry, it starts with a decision, followed by a massive, all-out action—a commitment to do whatever it takes, no matter how long it takes, to fulfill your greatest "why."

In my training seminars, I often talk about a trip that my wife and I took to China, wherein I found myself having to go the distance. It was one of the most incredible vacations that I've ever experienced; the entire event was absolutely wonderful, but getting the opportunity to climb the Great Wall of China was life-changing for me.

We arrived at the site one afternoon amidst crowds of people from around the world, all of whom had come to experience this incredible piece of world history. Thousands gathered at the bottom of the wall, excited and energized to make their way up its winding staircases, past its series of towers and all the way to the top. Looking up, I could see that some of the stairs were of different heights, and that some seemed to reach at least two feet. The entire journey up the wall had to be at least two miles, and those stairs didn't look too easy to climb.

But we went for it, and set out up the staircase. After climbing for a while, I began to notice that I had actually caught up with a few people who had started before me, and had passed others who had slowed down to rest. Some people moved at a relatively steady pace; some climbed slowly; others had stopped completely. Many had lost their motivation and desire to go forward.

I, however, continued to climb, although with each step, it was more and more difficult. I felt my legs, knees and ankles beginning to ache. I looked back to see how far I had climbed and saw the countless people I had left far behind me. The higher I climbed, the fewer people I noticed up ahead.

When I got to the sixth tower, I looked up to what I thought was the last tower, but suddenly saw one more beyond it. The top was further away than I'd originally thought. I stood there, exhausted, with nothing more left to give physically. I just stopped for a moment, gazing up at that final tower, which seemed miles and miles away. Every muscle in my body said, "Quit and be happy with where you are." But the champion in me said something different.

Paying no mind to my physical state, my mental attitude took over, and I remembered that I always played to win. I didn't want to have to tell the story about how I *almost* climbed the Great Wall, how I *almost* went to the top. I wanted to be the best and to do that I had to keep going. I closed my eyes and prepared for the rest of the climb. Then, I picked up my foot and took another step.

I decided that I would let my mental strength take me through the rest of the journey. Step by step, I ground it out, mentally blocking out the pain, chanting silently to myself, "I will *always* be at the top, I will *always* be at the top, I will *always* be at the top! Just keep it moving! Just keep it moving!"

With that final mental push, I opened my eyes and there I was—at the very top of the final tower. There were less than five people up there with me, leaving plenty of room for others who might come along.

My journey to the top of that wall is analogous to the journey toward the top of a network marketing opportunity. Many people get started with great enthusiasm, excitement and expectations. But as the journey goes on, unforeseen challenges and obstacles begin to unfold, and the climb becomes difficult. Some people eventually find it impossible to keep the steady pace that network marketing requires, and resolve to slow down or simply give up.

But those who are determined to see the top press on, with the understanding that in order to experience another level of success, more skill and mental fortitude is required. That's what this book is all about: providing you with information to help you acquire the skills and develop the proper mindset you'll need to make your way up to the top.

So, the question is, are you ready to take the journey? Or, if you have already started, will you go the distance? If not, will you just be another casualty who simply didn't finish the climb? One thing for sure is that every day someone makes it to the top. Have you made the decision that you're going to finish the climb?

Spencer's View

The Lawnmower Man

Developing a great work ethic and the drive to achieve success starts at an early age. As I was growing up in southern Georgia, I always wanted to make my own money. Sure, my parents would give us kids an allowance each week for doing our chores, but I was growing up in the era of Nike Air Maxes and Air

Jordans. These were not inexpensive shoes, and I had to have them.

My dad would always contribute $30 toward any pair of shoes that my siblings and I liked. His thinking was that we could get a brand-new pair of Converse Chuck Taylors for around that much, but if we wanted something more expensive, we would have to make up the difference.

Have you ever worn a pair of Chuck Taylors? For an athlete, their all-canvas construction provides no ankle support, and there's virtually no cushioning on the soles. It feels like you're walking barefoot. If I wanted to play sports—and I did—I knew I had to have something better.

So, what I began to do when I was twelve was find ways to earn money for myself. The first business that I started was a lawn service. I really took a lot of pride in my work. I would borrow my dad's lawnmower and go door to door throughout our neighborhood, asking if I could cut each homeowner's grass. I would cut the front, sides and rear of the yard, trim and bag the clippings and rake for $10 to $15. I figured out what to charge by calculating the amount of time I would spend on average with each yard, how many yards per day I could cut and how much gas I would need to buy to get to them.

Ten to fifteen dollars for a mowed and cleaned-up lawn seems like a good deal for the customer, but let me tell you, I put a lot of work into what I did. We didn't have a mower with traction control, so it was like driving a car with no power steering—it took a lot of effort. Some people would let their grass grow so high, the mower would stall out with each push, making that job last longer and taking time away from my next potential customer.

But I stuck with it, and my service became pretty popular around the neighborhood. Soon, I even developed some regular customers. Most of the time, I mowed lawns on Fridays and Saturdays. On Sundays, on the way to church with my family, I would ask my dad to slow down as we drove past a yard that I had just cut, and glow with pride as I pointed out the sharpness of the trim or how uniform the grass was.

Pushing that little mower on those hot summer days was where my love of earning money began. I did that for a couple of years, until a gentleman from our church opened up a brand new fish market and was looking for employees. I was still too young to be employed by a traditional business, but I thought that this was a perfect time to get my foot in the door nonetheless. I asked Mr. Johnny if I could work for him, and he agreed.

I appointed myself executive vice president of the fish cleaning division, managing one employee: myself. Though I was excited to have a "real" job at last, the work was the most disgusting thing I'd ever done. At the end of each workday, I would stink so badly that my mom would make me take all of my clothes off before entering the house.

People would come into the shop, particularly during the summer, when family reunions were at their peak, and order fifty pounds of catfish at a time, all filleted. Catfish is unique because it has a skin-like surface, instead of the scales found on most other fish. This meant that I couldn't use the high-speed electric scaler; instead, I had to manually peel the skin off of each individual fish before I could begin to filet it. This took a long time, but I always tried to do it as fast as I could—it seemed to impress the customers.

For all that work, I was paid $1 per hour. Needless to say, this was the job that taught me to respect the time and effort I put into it versus the amount of money I was paid. I worked there for just two weeks. To this day I have never cleaned another fish.

"Slave" for a Day
Southern Georgia has a strong agricultural economy and for decades it relied heavily on manual labor to keep its watermelon, cotton and tobacco fields alive. Working in the fields, when I

was a kid, meant good money for a young person. I had friends who were making $25 a day—they were rich!

Another gentleman who attended my family's church, Mr. Crawford owned a lot of land and grew several crops, but mostly tobacco. For years, I'd been asking him to let me work with the other guys and finally, one day, he said "yes"! I couldn't sleep that night, thinking about how much money I was going to make.

There were no official hours when you worked in the fields; you got there when the sun went up, and when the sun set, you went back home. On my first day of work, the old, flatbed truck that transported Mr. Crawford's field hands pulled up to my house at 5:30 a.m., and I was already dressed and waiting. I hopped in the back with the other "slaves" and soon was fast asleep, covered up with a dusty, burlap blanket.

When we got close to Mr. Crawford's farm, I was awakened by the truck's bumping along on the dirt road. I sat up just in time to notice that we had entered a clearing. Then, the truck stopped.

The "guard," who was also the driver, got out of the truck, slammed the door shut and said, "We're here. Everybody get out." I hopped out of the truck, looking around and thinking, *We're where?* In the blackness of the morning, all I could make out was a huge field, maybe 600 yards wide and just as long.

As we walked to the field, one of the other guys gave me a sixty-second training on how to pick tobacco: bend down, grab the big, fan-like blades of the pungent-smelling plant as near the stem as possible, place it into my bag and keep moving. Don't fall behind the rest of the workers because that means a long day for everyone. That was it. I was handed a bag, and off I went.

My first foray into the field was adventurous, to say the least. On summer mornings such as this one, there was lots of dew, which made the soil soft and muddy. On my first step, my shoe sank about a foot deep into the mud; when I tried to pull it back, the shoe was suctioned right off my foot. So, there I was with one shoe in the mud, trying to balance myself, already behind the other guys. I stuck my hand into the mud and extracted my shoe, and put it back on my foot, then got to work in the shallower parts of my assigned row.

Before long, it became apparent that the more tobacco I picked, the longer my row seemed to get. I was very athletic and strong, but my back began to ache something horrible about halfway down my row; the constant bending and picking just didn't agree with me.

On top of that, I had a terrible case of entomophobia—a fear of insects—and in that field, I saw some of the biggest, scariest-looking caterpillars, worms and flying creatures on earth! Between swatting gnats and watching out for snakes, I fell farther behind in my picking duties, but after three grueling hours, finally, we finished.

Whew! I thought. *This was tough, but not a bad day's work. I can do this!*

At that point, our guard came over and though I figured he would tell us to take a break after a job well done, instead, he gave me some of the worst news of my life: *We had only just begun.* It was only nine o'clock in the morning, and we had two more fields of the same size to complete before lunch. A small tear formed in the corner of my eye as I just stood there, incredulous as to what had just happened.

We worked until about one o'clock, when the sun was roasting us like rotisserie chickens at Boston Market. Then, we all piled into the back of the truck again and were driven back to the "plantation" for a one-hour lunch break. I remember that some of the other "slaves" had brought their own food in paper bags, and some were taken to the local convenience store for lunch. But not me! No, I was the minister's son, so I was summoned to "master's house" for my lunch!

Now, Mr. Crawford's wife was very ill at that time, and she

did not get out too much, but she didn't miss a beat when it came to cooking. When I entered their house, I was greeted by the smell of fried chicken. Sitting down at the table, I was also offered corn bread, homemade biscuits, collard greens, candied yams and sweet tea. I ate like I was an escapee on the underground railroad, led by Harriet Tubman herself!

Boy, was that a big mistake. It was soon time to get back to work, but my body had become so stiff from sitting in the air-conditioned home that I could barely move. On top of that, all the good food had made me terribly sleepy. When I boarded the truck, the rest of the "servants" looked at me jealously, probably thinking back to their own lunches of pickles, soda pop and MoonPies.

As we headed back to the field, I prepared myself mentally for more grueling hours of bending and picking, but then, to my surprise, the truck stopped. I was dropped off in a different area and told that I'd be a "racker" for the afternoon, working with six other people to process the tobacco. We would take the freshly picked leaves, place them on a spiked metal rack and press down on the rack until the spikes had penetrated all of the leaves and locked on the other side. Then, in teams of two, we would lift the rack and carry it into a drying shed, where the leaves would cure for a number of weeks.

I soon found out that this task was just as backbreaking as my morning's work had been. It was very depressing, too, because I had to listen to the conversations of my adult coworkers, many of whom had been doing this job for *years*, and supported their families solely through this work. Years later, I learned that this new task was actually a demotion for me; because I'd been so slow during the morning shift, I'd been assigned to this all-female battalion for the afternoon instead.

Finally, the sun went down and the old truck picked us all up. My body was beat; between the hot sun, the constant bending and the heavy lifting, I could not take any more. When the truck dropped me off at home, I practically fell out of it and staggered over to the side door of the house. I was so dirty that I had to undress outside.

I mean this with all of the honesty that is in my body: That day was, and still is, the longest day of my life.

But I had never quit anything before, and I did not want to start just then. So, I went inside, climbed onto the top bunk in my bedroom and like the biblical figure Hezekiah, turned my face to the wall and prayed the most sincere prayer I could think of: "Lord, if there is *any way* that I don't have to go to those fields tomorrow, or ever again for that matter, I would be forever grateful!"

After that, I instantly fell asleep.

The phone rang at four-thirty in the morning and woke me up. A few seconds later, my dad tapped on the door and whispered, "Mr. Crawford called and said that they're finished with all of the fields. He wanted to thank you for your help yesterday. You can go back to sleep."

Another tear formed in my eye. Who says God doesn't answer our prayers?

Now, years later, I learned that this was actually how they *fired* people who were no good at working in the fields. But from that single twenty-four-hour period, I had learned a lifetime's worth of lessons. I learned to be careful of what you ask for, because you just might get it. I learned that my body was clearly not built for intense manual labor, and that I must continue to excel in school and complete my education, lest I restricted my options in life.

A Real Job

When I turned fifteen, I was finally old enough to work for a *real* company. I was hired by a local steakhouse as a dishwasher and busboy.

This was a good enough job, but again, a busy one. Some nights, especially on the busy weekends, the dishes would pile up over my head, and I would be buried in suds and grime. But I would always make tasks like this a competition. I would challenge myself to see how quickly and efficiently I could clean the dishes. The more backed up I became, the more determined I was to get caught up.

But I had to take periodic breaks to bus or clean the tables for the wait staff. This, too, I tried to do as efficiently as possible. Instead of just carrying one container, I stacked two or three on top of each other, to reduce trips and quickly create more room for waiting patrons.

When I wasn't bussing or washing dishes, I was responsible for cleaning and wrapping potatoes. Boxes and boxes of them would be dumped into two huge sinks, where I washed them—hundreds of them—and then individually wrapped them in foil for baking. To this day, I can wrap a potato in aluminum foil in 1.3 seconds—it's almost instinctive!

The energy and determination with which I approached my many assignments eventually caught the eye of the restaurant owner, who promoted me to cook, and I was thrilled. I loved cooking, and tried to turn this job, too, into my own personal competition. I tried to prepare the most beautiful, succulent steaks anyone had ever seen. I even convinced the two other cooks on my shift to participate in daily competitions to see who could have the fewest returned orders and the most compliments.

On holidays, such as Mother's Day, Christmas and Easter, lines of people stood outside the restaurant, waiting to be seated, and I had to handle dozens of custom orders at a time. I had to remember which orders were first and which were last, what steaks were rare, medium rare and well done, who wanted special sauce and who wanted sautéed onions. To say the least, this job taught me how to multi-task like a pro, and to develop systems to handle information quickly.

This restaurant experienced its best years when my older brother, John, and I worked there. It came as no surprise that it went out of business a few years after we left to attend college.

What separates people who become super-successful in life from those who do not? That's a great question. I can tell you for sure that it's not how people look, what they wear, or even where they went to school. The single biggest common denominator among people who have "made it" is their *work ethic*. In this industry, this is why we tend to target entrepreneurs and business owners in our recruiting efforts—because these people are keenly aware of the value of their time and the commitment necessary to earn a living based solely on their own efforts.

Owners also understand the ebb and flow of business, meaning that they know that the only constant in business is change. They know that one month, they may have record sales and then earn nothing for the next few months after that. They also understand that there is a direct correlation between the amount of time they invest in their business and the return that they get—an important aspect of the dynamics of network marketing.

Nothing in life is worth having if you are not willing to do the work for it. The difficult road is paved with hard work and diligence, and used by champions. The easy road is paved with laziness and is overcrowded with losers and quitters. Which road do you want to take?

Avoid the Entitlement Trap

There is an entire generation of kids growing up right now who feel as if the rest of the world owes them something. This perspective is the by-product of laziness and a lack of discipline.

As The 3 CEOs, we call this the "entitlement trap" and, unfortunately, it plagues millions of adults as well.

The entitlement trap is nothing more than an enabler for excuses. Nothing is ever your fault. It's your coworker's or boss' fault that you didn't get the promotion. Your schoolteacher didn't like you, so you didn't pass the test. If your mother and father had fed you more oatmeal and given you more hugs, you would be more assertive as an adult.

To that, I say, whatever! When you really peel back all the layers of excuses, one simple truth is revealed: *We are not entitled to anything.* In business, you get what you deserve. You eat what you kill. Nothing comes to you for nothing, and the sooner you can rid yourself of this mentality, the sooner progress can be made toward reaching your goals.

The Haters

Going into business for yourself shows that you have qualities rarely found in the average person—that you are independent, a risk-taker, motivated, a visionary and a hard worker, among many other things. It shows that you have dedication, a solid work ethic and a drive to make something of yourself—to make your life better and more rewarding.

We all enter into the realm of business ownership presupposing that at the very least, the people we care about the most, our family and friends, will support us. But, oh, are you ever in for a surprise! Lurking in the shadows of your life are the people we affectionately describe as "the haters." These strange, mythical characters will smile to your face and say all of the things that they know you want to hear, like, "I hope your business does well," or "If nobody else buys from you, you know you can count on me!"

Yeah, right! What they're *really* trying to tell you is more like, "You'll be back at your nine-to-five with the rest of us in a couple of weeks," and "Why would I spend my hard-earned money to make *you* rich?" It's unrealistic to think that people really want us to succeed, especially when we're trying something new.

Novice entrepreneurs must understand that the haters are an absolute in business-building; they have always been around, and always will be. But they must also learn to do what already-successful entrepreneurs do, and use the haters as motivation to work even harder and achieve more goals. Like sports teams who post their competition's trash-talk in their locker room before a big game to get themselves all riled up, entrepreneurs should take the haters' words and use them as fuel, then go on and prove them all wrong.

To keep yourself motivated in the face of opposition, I recommend using daily affirmations. Every day, take a few minutes to read these lines while thinking about whatever haters you have in your life:

- I choose to succeed this day in spite of you.
- I choose to ignore your ignorance and embrace my enthusiasm.
- I choose to make constructive use of my free time.
- I choose to interact consistently with other positive, motivated people like myself.
- I choose to win this day because I am the best me that I know.

And, in time, those haters' words might not mean as much.

Run Like Rocky

In the first *Rocky* movie, Sylvester Stallone plays a club fighter who unwittingly gets a chance to box with the current world champion. In one scene, while he's training for his upcoming bout, Rocky gets up at four in the morning, drinks a protein-filled, raw egg shake and then, in the dead of winter, begins a long, lonely jog through the city of Philadelphia. As the scene progresses, he runs faster and faster, culminating in his famous, triumphant scaling of the art museum's steps.

The journey that you must make as an entrepreneur or successful networker will be similar to this motivational scene. Like Rocky, to get your chance to spar with the best, you must be willing to do the things that the average person will not. You must commit to those long, lonely nighttime or early morning drives to trainings and seminars; you must give every presentation your all, even when the audience is only half full. Not every moment will be a triumph, but even your worst days will bring you one step closer to your goal.

I remember how on one of our first tours through Florida, our first three stops, in Tampa, Orlando and West Palm Beach, were filled with excited anticipation. We had a wonderful opportunity and product, the timing was great, and relatively few people had heard about it at the time. I had packed my bag with a few hundred applications, just to make sure that we could quickly sign up the masses of people we expected to come to our presentation. I probably don't even need to say that only five showed up.

Talk about a letdown! If that tour did one good thing for us, it was helping us realize that this was going to be a long journey. We *weren't* going to build our business overnight, and we *wouldn't* be enjoying success right out of the gate. However, that tour also helped us prove to ourselves that we were willing to make the long-term commitment to ensure success.

This is the part of becoming wealthy that nobody tells you about, the part of it that you don't see. Success requires sacrifice. I have my own definition of this word. I define sacrifice as the difference between what you *want* to do and what you *must* do right now. Unfortunately, too many people are unwilling to forego what they want and ultimately miss out on tons of opportunities because they won't make the necessary sacrifice. You see, the physical manifestations of the work—the cars, the houses, the clothes, the lifestyle—are always evident, but the tireless and thankless hours that go into earning those things are not. Sometimes, you don't even realize they exist until you're in the middle of them, until you're taking those overnight road trips or making a hundred phone calls in a day. At those times, you have to just remember that there *is* a light at the end of the tunnel and that, like Rocky, you will have your day in the championship ring.

Remember Lot's Wife

The Bible tells a story about Sodom and Gomorrah, two cities that were so evil and wicked, God made the decision to destroy them. But first, He sent angels to tell a man named Lot to take his family and leave as quickly as possible. He would spare them, as long as they followed His only instruction: "Don't look back."

As Lot and his family were getting out of town, Lot's wife couldn't resist the temptation to turn around and see what they had escaped. Perhaps she needed to reflect upon what she'd be missing, or maybe plain old curiosity just got the best of her. Whatever the reason, she did look back at Sodom and Gomorrah and, for her disobedience, was turned into a pillar of salt.

In business, you must keep this story in mind because it is all-important to stay focused on your goal and to *not look back*. Sure, bad things are going to happen from time to time; you will experience setbacks and face challenges that seem impossible to overcome. In addition, many times, you will have to make choices that will affect your business for better or worse, and you just have to pick a side, then run with it. When you find a business or a cause worth fighting for, you have to go for it hard and fast, and never reflect on what you think you may have missed had you gone the other way.

The grass always looks greener on the other side, they say, and it's easy to become distracted by your competitor's lawn. Maybe it's better kept than yours, more verdant and more pleasing to the eye. But don't spend too much time looking back at what somebody else is doing; instead, spend your time fertilizing your *own* grass. In time, it will turn green, too!

Overcoming Obstacles

One year, Floyd, Donald and I planned a 3 CEOs five-city tour encompassing Charlotte, North Carolina; Baltimore, Maryland; New York City; Columbia, South Carolina; and Augusta, Georgia. We planned to do our presentations, meet a lot of people and, hopefully, come away with a lot of new team members.

Now, for some reason, our flights for this trip never got booked—a little detail we didn't know about until two days before we were scheduled to leave. At that point, we were faced with two options: cancel the tour and disappoint several eager leaders and team members, or find an alternative way to make the trip. Of course, we immediately chose option two.

Without hesitation, and without our team ever knowing, we loaded up Donald's minivan in Atlanta and drove to each destination on the tour. We're talking hundreds of miles here. Thankfully, there were three of us to split the driving and expenses; it sure wouldn't have worked out if we'd each been on our own.

At each stop on the tour, we changed clothes and brushed our teeth in filthy public bathroom stalls, then went into our presentations smiling and confident. No one ever knew that anything was wrong. The whole thing was a challenge—a mighty big one, let me tell you—and we could have come up with a million plausible excuses to just cancel the tour and stay home, licking our wounds. But, our individual and collective drives toward success wouldn't let us. We had to perform, no matter what the circumstances, because we would never reach our goals if we didn't. As they say, you can make money or excuses, but you can't make both.

We have countless stories like this—ones in which we slept in cars instead of hotels, or did back-to-back presentations with ten hours of driving in between. As The 3 CEOs, we've faced an awful lot of situations wherein the average person may have just given up. The difference—our difference—is that we kept right on going.

The race for success is won not by the person who runs the fastest, but by those who simply finish the race. View every obstacle that you face as another opportunity to test the limits of your faith in God *and* yourself, and you'll be amazed by what you can do. When you muster the resolve to push through the tough times that come your way, often you find success on the other side.

Family Tragedy

Some of my fondest memories from childhood are the times that I spent fishing on the lake with my grandpa. On these outings, he taught me not so much about fishing, but about life.

My grandmother and grandfather had a great, old house in Cleveland, Ohio, with a big front porch with a swinging bench seat. We would spend hours out there on long, summer nights, eating ice cream and talking about the Cleveland Indians, the Bible and our family. I treasure those memories; they are visions of intimate moments that can never be replaced.

During one of our 3 CEOs tour stops in Chicago a while back, my mother called to tell me that my grandmother had gone into the hospital to have a minor procedure done. At the time, Grandma was taking care of Grandpa, who had developed Alzheimer's. Many of my relatives in Cleveland had visited Grandma already, and her prognosis was good. When the surgery was through, she was smiling and talking, and asking when she was going to be released.

I was concerned about the hospitalization, but pleased that

she was doing well, and I boarded my flight from Chicago to Atlanta feeling pretty good about the situation. As soon as we touched down, I turned my cell phone on and found that I had several messages, as usual. One was from my wife, Tonya, and I could tell from the sound of her voice that something was wrong.

I called back immediately, but Tonya sounded better then, and didn't mention anything out of the ordinary. So, I asked to speak to my daughter, Hayley, who was four at the time. And the first thing she said was, "Hi, Daddy. GG's in heaven!"

My heart sank.

My hands and voice trembling, I asked Hayley to put Mom back on the phone, and Tonya finally told me that while I was in the air, a complication arose with my grandmother's recovery and she passed away unexpectedly. Tonya had wanted to wait until I got home to tell me in person.

I couldn't believe that just like that, my grandmother was gone, that I would never see her again, never taste her incredible caramel cake or hear her ear-piercing soprano at church. I would never get to tell her I loved her, and how much I appreciated her. I was devastated; I still have days when I miss her, and it makes me very sad.

Given the severity of my grandfather's Alzheimer's, it was difficult to tell if he knew that his wife of more than fifty years was gone. We all suspected that behind his sullen face, he knew, and less than sixty days later, he died, too. I was so distraught that I couldn't even attend the funeral.

In the midst of these family tragedies, not many people in my organization knew the pain that I felt or was going through. Because I knew that thousands of people were counting on The 3 CEOs to help them build their organizations and train, motivate and encourage their teams, I carried the sorrow in my heart, but did not allow the demons of pity and despair to deter me from moving forward. Life goes on, after all, and though the grief process must run its course, we must not let it run us.

When you experience difficult times in your personal life, do your best to turn them into platforms for triumph. Instead of giving in to despair, use what you feel to push forward, more strongly than ever, toward your goals, and work through the pain. I know that my grandparents would be so proud of the man that I have become, and I honor their legacy every day by practicing the values they instilled in me as a child.

Rejection

Some people cannot progress in an industry like network marketing because of an acute fear of rejection. If unresolved, this can become an obstacle that can really set you back.

But rejection is a part of life; we all hear "no" from time to time. And in network marketing, the odds are no different. Not everyone to whom you present a new idea or opportunity is going to be as excited about it as you are. That's okay; just remember to take the emotions out of your business barometer and understand that when people say "no," they're not rejecting you—they are rejecting the opportunity.

Of course, when this happens, it doesn't mean that you have to take it lying down. If someone declines your offer, take it as a challenge to prove that they made a big mistake by *not* joining you. Become successful in spite of their rejection and I guarantee that at some point, they'll see the error of their ways and join you. Get over it and get busy, and don't let rejection ultimately affect your progress.

Donald's View

Passing the Work Ethic On

When I was a kid, my parents had a few house rules: My siblings and I had to do our chores before we could go out and play; if we didn't finish our chores before sundown, there would be no playtime; and Saturday morning was for working, not for sleeping.

While most kids I knew were sleeping until noon every Saturday, I was up early, making sure that I did my share of the chores. As the youngest child, I often got the easy chores, the one that couldn't easily be messed up, like cleaning the bathrooms and taking out the trash. When I was a little older, I was put in charge of mowing the grass and sharing similar duties with my siblings.

As you can imagine, this sort of schedule wasn't a whole lot of fun for a kid. Don't get me wrong—I had plenty of time to play, and enjoyed my childhood a great deal. It wasn't all about scrubbing and mowing. But my parents always said that they didn't want to raise lazy kids, and so they set for us some high expectations—ones that we always strove to meet, and then exceed. In their own way, they taught me about the spiritual law of success early on in my life: Do more than what you're paid for so that later, you'll get paid for more than you do. This is one of the ideas that has gotten me to where I am today.

Because of my parents, I learned at a young age that I was responsible for doing my share as part of a team; I also learned the pride of a job well done. Though we weren't rewarded with money or other "perks," as we are now that we're adults, we learned how good it felt to do our best just to do it—not to please our parents or each other, but to please ourselves with our own sense of accomplishment.

This was the work ethic I was taught since I was old enough to comprehend the concept. Work before play, and do the best job that you can—this was what my parents taught me with their words and through example, for they were two of the hardest-working people I've ever known. And, I'm thankful that they did teach me that, because it is the basis of the strong work ethic that has brought me success today.

As a parent myself, I try to instill the same values in my children that my parents passed down to me. In our house, there are separate areas for work and for play, and the kids know which one comes first. If they choose to be on athletic teams at school, I make sure that they practice year-round, as I had done at their age, so that when game time finally comes around, they will not let their teams down.

I teach my kids all the same things about work and responsibility that my parents taught me, and I know for sure that I, too, will not raise lazy children. They will also become hard-working, intelligent adults who know the value of good, hard work, and they will find success in whatever they put their minds to.

In the network marketing industry, you can take these lessons to heart. Though I don't want to say that your team is like your family, there are familial aspects to it; to be successful, there must be a sense of teamwork, reliability and cooperation among your team, as well as a sense of camaraderie. After all, how well could a bunch of people who don't like each other work together?

And as their leader, you have to bring out the best in them work-wise. New team members should come into the opportunity with a pretty strong work ethic in place, but it's your job to reinforce that, to remind them to do the best work they can, and then to try to do better than that. Remember, network marketing is not just about making money; it's about personal development as well, and there is no better way to help a person develop than to remind them that they should work not for the applause or for the money, but for the work itself, and for the pride they can feel in accomplishing it.

Do It Yourself

Sometimes, for a variety of reasons, people do not have the opportunity to learn about work and responsibility early on in their lives. Later, as adults, they find themselves untrained in these areas. If you feel as though you did not learn enough about discipline and commitment in the past, don't despair—there is hope for you yet. These qualities, also known as your internal drive or your work ethic, can be developed later in life and used to help you reach the goals you desire.

The first step is, of course, recognizing that for whatever reason, you had inadequate support during your formative years. This isn't a value judgment on the person or people who raised you; you don't have to feel as though you're criticizing them or blaming them because you haven't made millionaire status just yet. All you're doing is acknowledging that there was something missing, and then working to fill that void.

Surprisingly, this is a difficult task for many people, especially those who did not have much responsibility when they were younger. Think about it: If something was missing from your life, how are you supposed to *know* that it was missing? I've seen people who were never required as children to get along with others and as adults, have found themselves without many friends, and they can't figure out why. Sadly, it's because they were not properly trained to interact with others socially, and so they have no idea how it actually should be done.

And the same can go for work. If work was never properly modeled to you when you were a child—by your parents or other authority figures—then how are you supposed to know how to do it? And if you don't know how to work properly and effectively as an adult, how can you ever hope to learn?

One of the best ways is to find a mentor or life coach who has achieved some of the things that you want for yourself. Look for a person who is successful in business, or who has something in general that you find appealing—more money, more time with their family, a satisfying spiritual life. Then, model your actions on theirs. Find out what made them successful and, as we've discussed before, emulate their behavior until you reach the same goals for yourself.

This is just another aspect of personal development, albeit a possibly tougher one than anything we've looked at before. I can say from experience that developing qualities and habits as an adult that you have not had all along can be difficult. Personally—and I realize that this is a problem that everyone should have—I've struggled to learn how to handle financial success. I grew up in a middle-class household, in a middle-class neighborhood; I wasn't used to excess money and once I began to have more coming in than I actually needed to stay afloat, I had no idea what to do with it. Because I was earning more money than my parents ever had, I had no previous model to follow. I had to find a whole new way to work with my finances.

To do that, I looked for new role models. I sought out people who had experienced financial success themselves, and looked at what they did with their extra income. Did they invest it? Did they buy bigger houses and cars? I looked at people who had not only nice things to show off their material wealth, but people who were smart with their money. I didn't want to blow everything I'd worked for on a mansion and a yacht; I wanted to pay for my children's college educations, and make sure that my family never had to worry about poverty. So, I looked toward people who had already achieved those things, and learned about what they had done to get there.

As I continue on my journey in network marketing, there are still things that I don't understand, things I have to learn about. But that's life, isn't it? It's one big learning process, a daily opportunity for personal development. Once you are no longer under your parents' or other role models' wings, you must continue to better yourself by looking for life coaches and mentors who can take you to the next level and teach you what you don't already know.

Of course, this doesn't mean that once you find a mentor, he or she will just tell you how it's done and that will be that. Being in a mentoring relationship requires a lot of work on your part as well. You must keep up with your coach—don't waste their time by not showing up for appointments or slacking off when they tell you what to do. Instead, show them that their lessons are heard and understood by using their information to get yourself closer and closer to reaching your goals.

This will not be a problem for people who are driven from within. These people never make excuses for their shortcomings but instead simply strive to improve them. They will not say, "My parents didn't teach me that, so I don't know how to do it." They *will* say, "I don't know how to do it right now, but I will find out and let you know!"

And that's the type of person you need to be to achieve success both in network marketing and in your life in general. No matter what obstacles are in your path, you have to keep going on your journey of personal development by conquering your biggest fears, having the self-confidence to succeed and not waiting for someone else to elevate you.

Afterword

Creating Your Dynasty

Proverbs 13:22 says it best: "A good man leaveth an inheritance to his children's children." This speaks to the importance of creating a dynasty, a legacy, for subsequent generations of your family, a means of assuring their future security—and your own peace of mind, because you will know that they will be provided for.

Network marketing has become a significant vehicle to create wealth and ignite the spark of economic freedom for people of all walks of life and socioeconomic backgrounds. We have used the leverage of this industry to generate income that our children's children will be able to benefit from for years to come. Network marketing is brilliant in this aspect because it uses the most sincere and direct form of advertising—word-of-mouth—to create a platform for earnings beyond your wildest imagination. By applying the lessons that you have learned in this book, we believe

that you, too, can discover your purpose and destiny and, ultimately, create a dynasty for you and your family.

The 3 CEOs believe that no other industry has leveled the
playing field for so many individuals as network marketing has,
and we invite you to join the ranks of those who have climbed the
ranks and become champions for themselves and their families.
We'll be watching as you make your ascension. We'll be at the
top, and we'll see you when you get there!